THE UNTOLD STORY OF THE REAL ME

Free Minds Book Club & Writing Workshop

Free Minds Book Club & Writing Workshop is a nonprofit organization that uses books, writing, and mentoring to empower DC youth incarcerated as adults to transform their lives and become powerful voices for change.

BOOK CLUB & WRITING WORKSHOP
Empowering young inmates to write new chapters in their lives.

Published by Shout Mouse Press,
a nonprofit writing program and publishing house for unheard voices

www.ShoutMousePress.org

The poem "18 to 42" was previously published in Tacenda Literary Magazine (2014)

Design by Tara Claeys, TLC Design

Cover Art by Ricardo Levins Morales

Photography by Renee Billingslea, Peter Broyles, Tanja Harambasic and Robert Lee

Free Minds Editorial Team

Tara Libert, Managing Editor

Kelli Taylor, Project Editor

Julia Mascioli, Project Editor

Calvin Minor, Editor and Free Minds Poet

Eddie Crist, Editor and Free Minds Poet

Phil Mosby, Editor and Free Minds Poet

Will Avila, Editor and Free Minds Poet

Maurice Beander, Editor and Free Minds Poet

Dedicated to the memories of
Free Minds members we have lost:

James

Cortez

Derrick

Christian

JohnQuan

Nadar

Andre

Darond

Dontel

Tyree

Antwone

And to all whose lives and families have been touched by violence. Our work continues in your names. We hope this book will take us forward in our quest to prevent future violence and heal pain in our communities.

And to the original Free Mind:

Glen

We believe in the power of reading and writing to teach, build community, inspire individuals and change lives.

CONTENTS

CONTENTS

CONTENTS

CONTENTS

CHAPTER 11 - A PENCIL IN MY HAND   108

CHAPTER 12 - TRANSFORMATION   114

CHAPTER 13 - THE COLOR OF MY SKIN   124

CONTENTS

Every week in a small classroom at the DC Jail, teenaged boys facing charges in the adult criminal justice system meet as a book club. For 90 minutes they travel beyond the cell walls, taking journeys to places both deep within themselves and far away across the globe. Most had never before read a book or written a poem. The 16- and 17-year-olds push beyond their comfort zones, engaging in discussions about books that often echo their own lives. Then they pick up pens to write about difficult feelings. Without their even realizing it, a powerful bond begins to form among them. As longtime member Will explains, "In (Book Club) we all had a feeling that we could somehow make it in life."

The first Free Minds Book Club session met in 2002. A year later, we held a public reading of the young men's writing. Family members and friends crowded inside a small café to hear their words. For many, it was the first time they had ever seen their young men recognized for something positive. The readings became a popular annual event requiring ever bigger venues for overflow crowds.

In 2011, the staff and members of Free Minds published our first literary journal, *They Call Me 299-359*, written and edited by young men serving sentences in federal prisons as far-flung as California, Louisiana, and New York. Initially, we envisioned sharing the book with people who wanted to learn more about our work. We would also send it to the more than 200 Free Minds members still behind bars to celebrate their own and each other's writing. Beyond that, we had few expectations. We did not know what a powerful teaching tool the book would become.

Soon after, with the help of members returning home from prison we created a violence prevention project called "On The Same Page." Calling themselves "Poet Ambassadors," our members take the book to audiences across the city hoping to protect other youths from becoming the perpetrators or victims of street violence. By reading poems and sharing their stories, they aim to give back to the community they once took from while also launching a vital dialogue on the root causes of youth incarceration.

Just as writing helped them to break down barriers in jail, the Poet Ambassadors now see it having the same effect in the community. Encouraged by the poems, students from tough neighborhoods who have been labeled "at-risk" and "behavior problems" open up, sharing stories from their own lives. A 7th grade boy asks the young men what he can do to keep his dad from going in and out of prison so that he can just be home with his family. A high school sophomore asks what she should say to her brother who she fears is running with a gang. Another boy wonders how to help his mom who is being beaten by a boyfriend. The poems encourage an honesty that melts away secrets and shame, as every one realizes he or she is not alone. Healing and understanding begin.

In the process, Poet Ambassadors profoundly change the way they see themselves. Once stigmatized by their charges, now they are the experts working towards positive solutions. They feel a strong sense of pride and purpose.

The sharing continues at Free Minds' monthly "Write Nights" where volunteers from across the community gather to provide written feedback and encouragement to the poets. The impact shows the power of writing to highlight the shared humanity of the writer and the reader. D'Angelo explains in a letter from prison:

> I was so surprised the first time I saw the comments! I didn't know people out there cared. When you come in here and you see you've been on the news, you figure people must be scared of you and no longer care about you. When I read what the people wrote on my poetry, I saw that they didn't think I was an animal, but just a human being who made a bad choice. It made me want to keep on writing!

The Untold Story of the Real Me represents the hundreds of poems written by our members over the last three years. It was edited by staff and a team of Free Minds members. The book's title comes from Free Minds member KB. Submitting a poem about his childhood ("Dear Brothers, I Remember When," p. 7) KB writes:

> When I first got locked up, I remember my mother telling me, 'Don't let your circumstances define who you are. You may be locked up but that's not who you are.' All I do is think of my life before the confusion, before the treachery, before the violence, ...Sometimes, while I'm walking on the compound I may smell something that takes me to a wonderful place! These nostalgic moments are the best moments I have. They remind me of the true person I am...this is the untold story of the real me, not the jail me.

As our Poet Ambassadors like to say, "Whenever a Free Minds poem is read, hope is spread!" Thank you for hearing these voices and gathering "on the same page."

Tara Libert and Kelli Taylor
Co-Founders

For My Fellow Brothers

By Michael

I would love to see you prevail
I hurt to see you fail
You deserve the best in life
I don't want you to live in a cage
Inside someone's jail
I wish for you to be free
I believe you can soar
Like an eagle high in the sky
Don't be afraid of being different
Or being called a *misfit*
When I imagine you employed
I feel like I wanna cry
Not tears of pain, but tears of joy
You are a king
The head and not the tail
I wish for you to be on top of the world
Two arms up
Screamin'
Brother, I made it!

CHAPTER 1

Photo by Renee Billingslea

GROWING UP

Charlie

When I was little I wanted to grow up and be a firefighter. My favorite possession was my toy fire truck. I lived with both of my parents. I knew that was unusual and I was grateful. I was kinda quiet, but I had my older brothers. We used to do everything together. Play football and basketball on our block all day long.

We were living in poverty though. We didn't have any money. I used to have hand-me-down clothes with holes in them, my brother's shoes, and old coats. So I used to get picked on in school. They'd be like, "You're dirty," and "You don't got the new Jordans." And then on top of that, I couldn't read or write that well. Every year, I just got left further and further behind. By the time I got to 7th grade I only had a 2nd grade reading level. It's kind of embarrassing to be in junior high school and you got to stand up in front of the class. I could barely read! That made me feel like, *I don't need to be here*. That's when I ventured off onto the streets.

All that playin' tag and swingin' on the swing set? All that just faded away. They call it "jumping off the porch." In the streets, they didn't care about my clothes. They was more into me. That's where I got my love from—the streets. I started to pick up the street ways. That led me into trouble. I started carrying a gun, robbing people. The path I was on led me to stop caring about everything and everyone. Then my brother got locked up. He was sentenced to 40 years. He was my best friend. I didn't care about anything any more. I was 16 and I thought I was being a man. Looking back, I wasn't a man. I wasn't doing anything but buying tennis shoes and new clothes. To be honest, I didn't really think I'd be alive to see the age of 21.

I know now what growing up and becoming a man really is. It's taking responsibility and being a family man. I go to school now and I'm not afraid to ask for help. I have a tutor. I also do outreach work with at-risk teens, so I can help them grow up the right way. My little girl is about to be a big sister. I want their childhood to be better than mine because I missed out on the entire experience of being a teenager. Going to regular high school, football games and graduation? I missed all of it. I can picture how it will be for my daughters. Me and their mom will be with them all the time, going to movies and having fun. When they are 16, they will get to see what being a teenager is supposed to be like.

I still sit on my stoop sometimes. I see a good future. I'm proud of what I'm doing.

Sitting on the Stoop

By Charlie

I was sitting on the stoop one day

When some cars came past my way

I was sitting on the stoop one day

When some girls came around my way

I was sitting on the stoop one day

When my mom came home one day

I was sitting on the stoop one day

When the police came and took me away

Now I don't know when I'm going to be home

But I know I'll be back again

Sitting on the stoop one day

Condon Terrace

By Mike

I come from a single parent home

Up the alley Condon Terrace was the crazy hood I roamed

Shoot out after shoot out

Police chase after police chase

Damn, when I look at it

My life was faster than Usain Bolt in that 500-meter race

Moms addicted to the bottle

Pops love the white

Every time I close my eyes

I saw those flashy lights

Don't move!

Get on the ground!

Chow time!

Inmate, tuck that shirt in them browns

Dear Brothers, I Remember When

By KB

I love moments when the aroma smells of things familiar
Of events lost in time
Like the pictures in Mama's photo books she keeps under the table
A collage of illustrations, stories with a simple label, *remember when*
When laughter and chatter filled the halls of our home
Light hearted, we sprinted into the day with youthful folly
That caused us to roam to the railroad tracks to imminent danger
Just to seek the thrill of no tomorrow
We jumped on speeding trains as if life, another we could borrow
Had death come, pain swiftly to follow
Our childhood would've been incomplete
But instead I remember when
When Dad's keys jingled, the tone of safely returned treasures and gifts
From a journey that seemed too hard
Sweaty and fatigued, he would still applaud at our childish antics
And briefly disregard, that our bedtime had passed and a new hour drew near
Listening, lending an ear to our discoveries of life
And what we wanted to be when we grew up
I remember when
When morning came too soon as if the night was bullied for some of its time
Mama it's too early, we would protest; she'd respond, *Quit your cryin'*
Spirituals filled the air with something only Sundays could bring
Fragrances of joyful noises, melodies
As Mama would sing her gospels all the way down the road
Onward to the proverbial lecture
The man in the gaudy robe would tell of heaven and hell
We'd say, *Mama how are our souls for sale?*
I remember when
When family gathered with greetings of smiles and hugs
Though trouble haloed over every head
The grill burned burgers and dogs
And while the sun descended the elders were looking ahead
The future, someone would begin, pointing to the young'uns in food-stained shirts
Once the authoritative speech had ended
We would laugh and cherish that fleeting moment for all its worth
I remember when

Puddles of Water

By Doug

The sun blocks my thoughts
But when it rains they roam free
I'm a victim of circumstance
Around people that don't know me
Maybe if they went through what I did
Things would be different
Moms working three jobs
Youngest sis' raising children
I thought people was trippin'
When they said things'll get better
'Cause they was wearing winter coats
And I was wearing a sweater
Refusing things Moms wanted to give
All I wanted was love
Trying hard to be a man
But misunderstood for a thug
Maybe I would change a few things
If I could go back
Moms would be smiling instead of crying
Yeah, I'd like that

I Once Was A Rascal

By William aka King X

Yeah, I once was a rascal

Cuz coming up in the hood was a hassle

Make it out, boy, I have to

Cuz the pillars are falling

And people move in procession

So I'm askin' the question

Was I really destined to use words as my profession?

My thoughts and my words clash

Hear the percussion

Still got a lot to learn

You can say I'm under construction

My mind is still thinking mayhem

But my heart beats rhythm

I try and speak solemn

Cuz I'm in the right row, just the wrong column

So I combat the problem

Or canvass this rascal

Cuz he's too much of a hassle

Life Story

By Alonzo

Teacher, how do I start my life story?
Should I start when I popped out my mother in 1994
Or do I start on the day when my father walked out the door
Maybe I'll start on the playground
Where ears were covered to block out the gun sound
Where a body could be found where I played
And police harassed me and my friends all day
Writin' my life in poetry is hard, Teacher
If you have nowhere to start
Wait I can start....
When I slept with the bathroom light on
Because I was scared of the dark
Or when I got beat up in the park
Because I wouldn't share my chalk
Or how I was laughed at in school
Because I wore shoes with no socks
Teacher, how do I write poetry 'bout my life?
When half the time I don't know
Where me and my family goin' to sleep at night
Or am I going to make it to sunlight
Okay Teacher, hold on, I got it, get ready to take notes
Starting at ten
When I seen crack addicts asleep in the hallway
High off the drugs they smoked the previous day
When teachers in school called me dumb
Because of my test grades
How do I start my life story?
When I can start from so many places
Teacher, you pick where to begin
Like your favorite food on a menu
Until then my life story is to be continued....

Over the Years

By D'Angelo

Over the years, I've learned about the people who fought

The people who weren't people

But property to be sold and bought

Over the years, I learned about the people who cried

Over the years, I've thought about the things I seen

You'll have to live in my shoes to see what I mean

Over the years, I've thought about the things I've done

Laughing and joking like everything was fun

I often think about the time I wasted

Instead of getting high, I could've gotten an education

Out of all the battles I fought, I was fighting for nothing

But as the old saying goes, you'll fall for anything

If you don't stand for something

Now That I'm Grown

By NC

I was bad with long dreads

Just seven years old

I admired my stepfather

This is messed up – he was in jail

I thought all real gangstas went to jail

I'd go visit him

Damn, that's a real gangsta, I thought

Now that I'm grown, I admire my mother

She do everything right

She's never been to jail

She finished school

Perseverance and loyalty

These are the qualities I admire now

My Nine Months Is Up

By Nick

I have waited what has seemed to be forever
For the day that I must be born
This small body of mine doesn't want to leave this isolated womb
But my mind is telling me that there is a different and better world
Outside of this mother whom I haven't yet met
I bet she is going to be the best mother of all
She has been feeding me whatever I desire for these past 9 months
I can't wait to be taught everything that she knows
I wanna know about the earth, Mother Nature, my nationality
And those who have sacrificed their lives
So my generation can have freedom
And when I'm born, I hope to see the open arms of my father
Whose duty is to spend as much time with me as possible
I hope that he teaches me to overcome
Because it will kill me if I become a statistic
I don't wanna end up selling drugs
Just because I wasn't taught any other way to be independent
I don't wanna gang bang against my own culture
Just because I was taught that was the only way to solve a problem
I don't wanna end up being somebody with a thousand excuses
For why I haven't got an education and a job
And I would hate the most to end up too indolent to think for myself
And expect things to get done by wishes and hope
I want to be strong not just physically but also mentally and spiritually
I want to be a leader and not a follower
I want to be a man who fights for what he believes in
A man who knows his creator (God)
And last of all I want to be a father and a husband
Who knows how to cherish his children and wife
Because a man with many children and a good wife
Is a man with many blessings
And a good life

Southeast DC

By Arthur

I am from a place where nobody wants to go because of poverty

I am from a fatherless upbringing, which is common in my eyes

I am from where grandparents raise their grandkids

I am from where people's morals are backwards

I am from where people worry about the new Jordans and not the light bill

I am from where prison is almost mandatory (sounds farfetched, but it's true)

I am from where everybody wears kufis, but don't practice their religion

I am from where death is common

I am from where you have to look over your back 24/7 to be on point

I am from where public schools pass you without attending class

I am from where teachers are drug addicts

I am from where being African American with dreadlocks is almost everyone

I am from where mistaken identity is highly possible

I am from where people need help but don't get it

I am from where you can't be weak or you'll stick out

I am from where the smell of gun smoke is usual

I am from where people eat in the dark

I am from where playing tag in the alley is fun

I am from where basketball hoops are made out of milk crates

I am from where you got holes in your shoes and clothes

I am from where you grow up too fast

I am from where every neighborhood has a candy lady and a bootlegger

I am from where Go-Go music is blasting from everybody's radio

I am from where babies are out at midnight

I am from Southeast DC

CHAPTER 2

Photo by Renee Billingslea

FAMILY

Gary

My mom was strung out on drugs when I was born. She left me sitting in a dirty diaper on my grandparents' doorstep. I didn't meet her until I was 12. I used to think about her though and miss her. Whenever I cried, I'd yell, "I want my Mom!" My grandparents would say, "Well, she's not here. We're here!" And that was that. When other kids would ask about her, I was embarrassed. I used to say my mom was dead.

When I finally met her, I felt so mixed up. On the one hand, I was angry. Like, she thought she could just suddenly show up after 12 years and be my mom. But then, she was nice to me and she bought me new shoes. That felt good, like, *Yeah, my mom's finally here.*

When I was locked up, I started studying Islam. The Quran says we should never disrespect our mothers. I learned about forgiveness. I realized that you only get one mother, so I forgave her. I started calling her and she came to see me. I understand now why my mom did what she did. To this day, I try to explain to my little sisters that she was doing her best. They still don't understand, but they will.

I don't know too much about my father. I don't know if he's dead or alive. I met him just twice when I was small. I heard a story that he left me in a bathtub one time when I was a baby. They say I almost drowned.

My life so far? It's makes me want a strong family that's united together. But it also makes me want to be patient. I'm not rushing to start a family until I feel as though I'm ready!

My family made me who I am. Everybody needs a family. Even if they're on drugs or whatever.

I wrote "A Mother's Love" when I was in the hole.* I remember, my mom was stressin' and goin' through some stuff. So I sat down and I wrote this poem for her.

---

* *The hole refers to solitary confinement. Gary was on solitary confinement for two years.*

A Mother's Love

By Gary

Mother, paradise lays at your feet

How indebted I am to you for the nourishment to eat

Mother, how powerful your name

Oh, how strong your frame

Strong enough to overcome your addiction

To see your son grow up

Yet weak for falling back into society's stereotype

Mother who carried me for 9 months in your uterus

Shielding me from harm in your own way

Only to inject me with the same poison

Still a queen to whom I give a throne of your own

Even after all of the broken promises and lies

Mother who left me wrapped at my grandparents' door

I know the cravings called and you had to run to get more

You left me so that I would never see you weak

But Mother, you never retrieved me…

How can I truly be angry—you carried me for 36 weeks

Starving yourself to make sure I'd eat

Mother, paradise lays at your feet

How strong you are even when you are weak!

A way to say thank you for your love

Is all that I seek

Always Had My Mother

By Antwon

I seen my mother go through withdrawals

I smelled the heroin coming out of her pores

There was days I had nothing

There was nights I had nothing

But my mother

We used to pray for better days

Momma always made a way

There was times I didn't have no food

There was times I didn't have fresh shoes

But I had my mother

Momma always held strong

She never worried that my father was long gone

There was times I couldn't get love from my own kind

There was moments that I second guessed my own friends

But I always had my mother

Make Them Smile

By Marquael

I wish I could give my mom my freedom

Walk out the jail gates then I see them

My grandma and my moms

Holding them in my arms

Heart racing, feeling alarmed

Mom cries tears of joy

Happy to see me, her oldest boy

Now I'm feeling real proud

To once again make them smile

Memoirs for Mother

By Ahmad

A woman fair skinned

Able to toil through a caste system

A woman with vestiges of pain

Still from the birth and tending to six beautiful children

A beautiful woman from a family of five siblings

Able to withstand, undergo, no matter how egregious the situation

My blood, sweat, and tears shed in dedication to the joy of this lady

Through her eyes my reflection

How my life she has affected when I drifted wrongly

Steered me always in the right direction

Though the mischief in me has not always succumbed

I still feel remorse for all the wrong that I've done

I stand before her humbled as any man before his mother

The gates of paradise at her feet

To one day bring her eternal happiness I pray

That she'll one day be able to see

That all my shortcomings should not be accounted for by her

But instead by me

My Loving Mother

By Elijahwon

My mother got so much on her mind

That she wants to cry

But she smiles

She tells me to do good

But I only do it for a lil' while

She always tells me about the world

Like Obama and a lot of interesting history I don't know about

She don't like the music I listen to

Because she don't want me to be around dat stuff

She gets mad at the lil' things

Cause if you can do something little

You can do something big

She always tells me, *Be thankful for what you got*

Like her and my family

Even though she don't have nothing to give me when I need stuff

She gives me love and I move on with my day

She's smart, strong and loving and caring for others

Even though I did something I wasn't supposed to do

She is still with me like a mother do

She wants the best for me

Like going to school

She always tell me, *Leave the street alone*

It's not for you

'Cause I am smart and loving and caring

And I say, *I got it from you*

I love my mother with all my heart

It's time I start doing something

Before I can't do nothing

What I Wish For You, Mom

By Zackary

I would love to see you proud of me
I hurt to see something happen to you
You deserve the best
I wish for God to look after me and my family
I don't want you in a bad place
I wish for you to enjoy life
I believe you can do that like anybody else
Don't be afraid to do what you like
And let me make money the positive way
You are a hard working woman
That loves me and my brother
I would love to see you proud of me
This is what I wish for you

Pain Grows in the Heart

By Malik

It started with a little hole in my heart

Running around in dirty diapers

Wishing it was food instead of rats

In the house with Momma

Wishing the crying would stop

But she don't know

About the pain growing in my heart

As I get older

The pain get uncontrollable

Wishing I was in the center of my mother's arms

While she reads my favorite book to me

But instead she's doing a double shift at a restaurant

When she should have gone to school from the start

Because she don't know about the paining hole

That's halfway in the center of my heart

People teasin' me

Because they see disbelief in my eyes

But all along it's tearful, tired eyes

Waiting for the painful hole

To stop growing in the center of my heart

Now I am older

So Momma gave me money, food, and clothes

But still no family to love

Until one day, Momma quit her job and came home

She couldn't give me no money, food, or clothes, just a hug

All it took was a hug

And the painful hole stopped growing above

You Are More To Me...

By Antwone

Mom, you are more to me

Than anything in the whole world

Without you, it's like not having no air

Without you, I wouldn't even be here

They say the biggest star in the sky is the sun

But I think otherwise

I think you is the biggest star

You are more important to me

Than the trees that give off oxygen

Sometimes I pretend to be the person that I'm not

You always told me

That you believed in me when I didn't

I do know right from wrong

But the pressure from this generation is just so strong

It's like I'm in the ocean getting taken by the current

I wasn't strong enough

But it's never too late

To make you happy

It's never too late

To be the rose that grew from the concrete

Mom, like I said

You are more to me than anything in the whole world

This poem is for you

To believe that

Antwone was killed on May 19, 2014

Visiting Hours

By Sammie

Anxious for the moment

While sadness eats inside

Looks deceive reality

Our hearts deeply cry

Smiles like sunshine

Knowing it's pouring down rain

Behind our expressions

We feel each other

She stays strong by day

And breaks down by night

I feel pain all day

But stand tall like height

So much runs through our minds

But only little is said

She knows I'm alive

But feel the situation dead

Emotions run through our bodies

Tears she begin to shed

My eyes began to water depress

I drop my head

Face-to-face with fear

Seeing the person who carried me nine months cry

Having me so tongue-tied

My mouth open, but I can't reply

One minute left, clock reaching end of the line

We just witness the moment

Until the next time

Memory I Can't Forget

By Kevin

I remember it like it was yesterday…but it wasn't

I was in juvie facing five years

When my little sister was killed

I was melting like ice in water

It looked as if it was over

I heard my family crying

It sounded very painful

The smell of death filled the air

I could taste nothing

It was like I was dead

I felt like I was in another world

I will never forget my sister in that casket

I remember because I love her

I can never forget

My Uncle

By Jerome

My uncle is addicted to drinking

Sometimes it's hard to predict what he's thinking

The little respect I have for him

Is slowly but surely shrinking

I hate to really admit it

But lack of love was the reason he did this

Even though he be trippin' I still love 'im

That wouldn't ever stop me from huggin' him

Everybody gave up, think he's gone

But I'ma be the one to prove 'em wrong

Before and After

By Brandon

Before

My little brother was burned in the fire

After

I had felt that life would not get better

I felt that no one could have a better brother

I acted as if I lost my best friend

I wished I never had to experience this

I just wish I had one wish

Dad

By Dre

Dad of the world

You got a boy

You was in

Then you was out

You came back 17 years later

Thinkin' I would love you

I think it's too late

A good man

Is already above you

Never Forgotten Dad

By Sharod

My father is not around

So me, I'm walking around DC

Sad, with my head to the ground

Trying to do right

Always seem to do wrong

Trying to find my happiness

Wanting to be the old me

I'm a diamond in the dirt

That never been found

I'm a rising king

That will always be crowned

Ghost Dad Part Two

By Juan

Hey you, snap out of it you got mail
The chubby CO* said, reminding me that I'm in jail
I wonder who wrote me, he never stops to put mail in my cell
Rip it open, Idiot, my conscience yell
I'm still playing the guessing game because nobody writes me
But it may be someone from my Free Minds family
So I look at the name and my body lights up
It's my dad and according to the address he's no longer locked up
My body starts to shake and my emotions are running deep
Not able to wait, I rip it open and take a peep
It's a picture of him inside and he looks just like me
Only difference is he's lighter and I'm almost 6 feet
So I read, *Hey son, how are you, I love you and I hope you love me*
I'm going to look out for you when I get out, you'll see
I'll visit you and if you need it I'll send you some money
I'm sorry for all the wrong I did, I hope you forgive me
I just wanted to let you know that I always loved you
And when we get out it's a whole lot of catching up we need to do
So here's my info and with it you can call Pops
I felt like a kid again chasing behind dad with fast bunny hops
I love you son and keep your head up
He wished me farewell and good luck
I read the letter 4 or 5 times before going to bed
Really not knowing why I still believed what he said
He just got released two days ago is what the letter read
So in the morning the phone is where I headed
I raced out of my cell disregarding hygiene
I dialed 301-271-**** and heard the phone ring
Welcome to Pizza Hut, can I take your order?
My heart sunk and my tears were at its border
So I let them fall and sobbed but not loud
And let all my emotions drip in a place where that's not allowed
Damn, why did I let him play me?
I was stuck there looking all crazy
Never again can I let him hurt or break me
Because I'm a strong young man who was raised by a lady
Thinking of the dad I wanted, but never had
This is part two of my life dealing with a Ghost Dad!

*correctional officer

27

Photo by Renee Billingslea

PARENTHOOD

Will

One day, when I was eight years old, my mom told me she was going to McDonalds. She promised to bring me back a Happy Meal. She never came back. I found out later that she went to be with another man and start a new family. I saw her on the street one day, and she pretended not to recognize me.

My father taught me a lot of things. I learned from him how to be a hard worker and a good provider. But I didn't learn how to open up emotionally. My father, he chose alcohol to erase his pain. He chose alcohol over his children. Then later on, he chose church to erase his pain. And he chose church over his children. If we didn't go to church, he disowned us.

I never pictured myself becoming a father. Mostly because I knew what I had chosen in life and I didn't want to expose a child to all of that negativity. I used to tell people that even if I did have a kid, I would never change.

It was Super Bowl Sunday last year when my girlfriend told me she might be pregnant. I went to CVS to buy a pregnancy test, but we decided not to take it until half time. I knew immediately. I could see it in her face. I was freaking out but I tried to be calm for her. I joked around. That's my defense mechanism. People are always telling me now that I'm a leader and a good person, so I told myself, *You can do this. You just have to take the first step.* But I was a little worried. Okay, a lot worried. My past is what scared me the most. Coming from a gang-infested neighborhood, I just didn't want my child to be like me. I chose the streets. And all the streets did was breed pain in my family.

Our son Dylan was born last September. I saw him and suddenly it was all real. I could actually see my whole path. Before I got locked up, I never even thought about my future. Now with Dylan, I've got this extra push to be more. He's my future and I want to be prepared. More than anything, I just want Dylan to know family and to know God. As long as he watches me and his mother, one day he will know God. I know I have potential to be so much and he's always going to be learning from what I do. So I'm just trying to be honest and humble and keep a smile on my face.

Hope = Dylan

By Will

What is it that I dream for anymore?

My freedom, my life, or maybe the thought of redemption?

I consider myself blessed at points

But condemned at others

I have survived the walk with those of the forgotten

I have survived the fights with the demons that I saw in my past

But I still felt lost, at times abandoned

My first reaction to see you was I hope that my sins won't carry on

Our first hug was a prayer for forgiveness

For all that you will soon witness

I see you and we lock eyes

I am blessed

You only consider me a man with the clear baby bottle

Trying to keep your head up until you get stronger

But to me, I see the faith of those that linger around church

To me, I see those who prostrate for another chance at forgiveness

When I see you laugh, all the pain, all the challenges disappear

All I see is innocence

I feel like the world stops

And I have been given a chance to make someone smile instead of hate

A chance to create peace

I just hope you never lose that laugh

Hope for you to be just you

Because "just you" has made my hope for a better man come true

My Savior

By Gerald

Who knew it would be you to save my life

My adorable son

To open my eyes and reveal my childish ways

You helped me rediscover myself

Now I'm countin' the days

Til I get back to you, fascinating little boy

You fill me up with so much joy

You're such an exceptional son

You don't know it, but I'll be home momentarily

It's an honor to be your father

An' I shall do my job perfunctorily

It was you who turn this boy into a man

Your father is your enormous fan

I love you kid, you're my greatest achievement

Your birth surpasses any accomplishment

You symbolize a younger, charismatic and innocent me

An' I shall protect you from everything I turned out to be

You accomplished something that no one could ever do

You made me grow up

You made me accept my responsibility to be a father

Your life is under my protection

So I'm your personal warrior

You already saved my life

So I consider you...My Savior!

Ma'ziyah

By Rico

Ever since you've been in my life
Hasn't been a day or hour you haven't been on my mind
I get an unexplainable feelin'
Lovin' you and knowin' you all mine
At only 8 months now, your smile and laugh alone
Make my life just shine
And for anyone to say you isn't
One of the most beautifullest babies that they ever saw
They will be lying!
Ma'ziyah, you is the air I breathe
The earth I walk on and the heart that's in my chest
I never thought I could love so strong
I feel something in my heart that was never there
At first I was livin' life not carin' about livin' or dyin'
But you have given me a reason to forever care
You is daddy's princess and I'm so glad
And I will always be by your side
To help you through whatever
I'm going to promise you
I will change for you and do better
And no matter there or not, dead or alive,
It will always be, *I'll see you later* and never *goodbye!*

I Want You to Know

By Delonte

Bundle of joy

Beautiful baby boy

I want you to know the sky is the limit

We got Obama and I got you

I know I mess up sometimes

You will learn that's what humans do

Just know daddy loves you

When you hurt, I hurt

When you need, I need

Right now you don't understand

But I hope when you do I will be there

And all of your childhood memories of me are fond

Not like mine

I never knew my dad

And he ain't know me

This is something I don't want to repeat

I fought so hard to get a street name

A little bit of street fame

But you have my last name

My blood

Just know Daddy loves you

My Son

By Devanta

If I have a son

I'm goin' to give him

Everything I didn't have

Like a father

CHAPTER 4

Photo by Renee Billingslea

THE STREETS

Juan

When I was younger, my impression of the streets was always glitz and glamour. It was the good life. Like a fashion show. The bad side—the heartaches, the pain, the suffering—that was all hidden. You only see the money, the cars, the clothes and the girls. It's all power and respect.

I never thought I'd end up in the streets because I had always been one of those kids who thought outside of the box. I was curious about the world outside of my neighborhood. But one time when I was in middle school I got suspended. I remember spending the whole day just roaming the streets and takin' it all in. It opened my eyes. I'd been put out of school that day, and suddenly I felt I was part of the streets—something I never thought I would be.

When I got to high school, I became what we call a red case. A red case means I did everything I was supposed to do at school. I did my homework, got good grades and played sports. But as soon as I stepped across that threshold, I was a different person. I was leading a double life.

I think so many young people are in the streets because it seems like an easier route than staying in school. A lot of them are neglected. Their parents are busy working two jobs, or chasing their addiction. These kids are just looking for a sense of family and belonging and they find it in the streets.

My dad constantly got locked up during my childhood. When he would get out, he always promised he was coming to pick me up. I would get so excited, but my dad was always a no-show. But I had a good mother and family that gave me love. For me, the trouble was misunderstanding loyalty. I caught myself being too loyal to my friends, and not loyal enough to myself and my family.

Now that I'm out, the young people around my way listen to me. All of the other brothers my age are either dead or locked up. But the young kids see me trying to do right and they wanna listen. They are just looking for someone to tell them what they should do. I see their wheels turning. I tell them, "If you can survive in the streets, then you can make it in school. Go to school! That's where all the girls are! You want to act the class clown, but that girl not gonna wanna talk to you if you're acting a clown and running the streets. She knows pretty soon, you're gonna be asking her for a dollar! She wants to talk to someone who is getting his education, because she knows he already got a dollar!"

Since I was little, I always wanted to be a lawyer. Now I'm thinking either that or a journalist. But maybe I will become a social worker, so I can keep helping these kids.

The streets will always be a part of me. I don't mean that in a negative sense. I mean that I will never forget where I came from and will always remain humble.

Da Struggle

By Juan

Kids starving, momma nodding and pops foreign

These are the broken homes that most of us were born in

No food, no heat and no water

This here is poverty where life expectancy is much shorter

No shoes, holey clothes and runny noses

In a place where praying is unheard of and who is Moses?

Prostitutes, drug dealers and cold killers

Doing errands for them so I can eat is all I remember

Birthdays was the worst day

We stole out of stores when we was thirsty

They say that it ain't no love for the wicked

But don't judge us, life chose us—we didn't pick it

Surrounded by steel fences, none of them pickets

It's like we were raised for jail; I don't get it

Kids getting used, molested and abused

Wearing long sleeves to school to hide the bruise

M.O.B., a lot of dudes say they live by the rules

And the young girls think it's cute but they are so confused

I love where I'm from, don't get it misconstrued

Even back when my lil' bro was crying from hunger

And I ain't know what to do

Years later and it still draws emotions from you

It's still taking our young men to jail by the bundles

I'm a proud survivor of the world that we call the jungle

And even when I get old and rich I'll always remember "da struggle"

This Superstitious Relationship

By DeCario

I can't understand why, but I love you

You show me signs on every corner

But still I adore

It's this unconditional satisfaction you bring me with joy

I wanna understand more

Should I call you sweetheart or my sweet mistress?

My girlfriend and family don't want to understand

My reasons for being with you

Like a junkie for some crack, I find myself going back

Unable to live without you

Is it the way the lights glow on us?

You got me hypnotized

But should I desire your presence?

And lose my girlfriend and family

I find myself superstitious in love

So deeply in love

The fame equals pain

The name equals hate

The life equals death

Are we blind to the facts?

She sees us ball

She sees us fall

You can call her "The Streets"

Our down fall

Claim

By Christian

When I'm home
I claim my loved ones
Claim my mother, father, sisters, brothers, and family
But when I'm on the street
I claim a dingy old red flag
When I'm with mi familia
I'm a different person
Just like how a pitbull
Is different around its owner

The Streets' Favorite Calls

By Deon

The power, the struggle
The muscle, the hustle
The streets' favorite calls
To me, kinda crazy
Why'd they call me?
But when I didn't respond
They screamed to me and cried
Letting the cries knock on my door
So attractive, everyone adored
I walked the streets on a collar
Making sure she slept, ate and survived

Promises

By LB

Endless fame and a pot of gold is what he promised for your soul

All you have to do is hold the Glock and slang that crack rock

Glistening diamonds and girls to go

But this life goes deeper

All you have to do is be a deceiver

Make a crack head a believer

Sell death to your people

But what happens to "I am my brother's keeper?"

Do you keep your brother down so you can get paid for a pound?

You cook your beef with a hundred rounds

So you think you should wear a crown

But they didn't tell you someone's bigger and someone's badder

Or when you fall in love that someone else had her

But now you want to fight 'cause you love her

So you step wrong

And never make it home

This is what happened to my man Thomas

But all along, that was the street's true promise

This is Our L.I.F.E.

By MA

I know cats that done rocked more dudes to sleep than a nursery

Baby Girl cried her life away screaming, *Stop Dad, you're hurting me*

Young Boy's birthday wish that his pops was here to see

Shawty's motha shot dope for the first time and she over-D

Lil' Slim showed his man a gun and said, *I'm hungry let's find something to eat*

Old Timer posted on the block, his pockets swollen like he just hit the lottery

Da Youngsta' dropping out of school

Thinks countin' money is more important than learning to read

Lil' Mama 15, can't even spell sex

But she's introducing this world to a seed

It's suppose to be Lil' Man's first year in college

Instead he got a full scholarship to do 50 in a penitentiary

Nowadays police jumping out on kids who's still in elementary

Every day this the life we lead in the streets

Either you survive and make it out, or

You D-I-E!

This is our L.I.F.E.

Nightmare

By Gary

Damn…

Screeching tires, then guns spitting fire

An ambush in the making

The heart is now thumping, the blood is now pumping

This moment is breathtaking

Begging for survival while running from rivals

Chased by the demons of death

Hating this part

Wanting light for this dark

Wishing other options for myself

Scenes of life flashing

Are mentally bashing

Now that you've recognized faults

Stopped in your tracks

From a blast in the back

As your body falls slow to a halt

The blood from your birth

Is now leaking in the earth

And the soil is now returned to its place

The heart and mind have expired

And that last look of life on your face

No words before leaving the families now

Grieving, saddened by the sudden surprise

They're stuck with a pain that forever remains

As you watch and shed tears from the skies

Damn I was dreaming…

In The Land of Opportunity

By CM

In the land of opportunity
I'm at a standstill like scarecrows
I remember back in the day
When I had to share clothes
Too many nights with no lights
And the bed cold with no heat
So we had to sit near a stove
Damn…
I still remember them days
Moms had a lil' job
But it was minimum wage
As a young'un I was street smart
But not as good at the grades
Why you think it's called "the trap?"
'Cause the hood is a MAZE!
I was pushin' quarter pounds of dat pack
Tryna prosper in poverty
A part of me purposely perpin'
So please pardon me
Police be tryna bother me
People tend to push me
I wasn't thinking logically
That's when dem' people took me
Now I'm trapped in a cage
In the land of opportunity
And it's kind of sad
'Cause things are better in here
Than out where I used to be
No way out
My opportunities are bare
Hoping that when I'm free
The land will still be there

Code of the Streets

By Drew

Raised to go hard, matter of fact

They said ain't no sympathy for the weak

Gunfire through Mommy's window

Moment of silence killed the kid in his sleep

Police investigate, please nobody dare to speak

Got the family wondering why

It's the code of the streets

Far from modest, lil' homie was promised college

He had a mean down low game

Colleges thinking next Rasheed Wallace, he was proper

But the boy had problems

Drugz, money, girls, plus rival gangs had him bothered

They killed his brother in a drive by, so he gotta settle the beef

He did him, judge gave him 60 for the code of the streets

Listen, lil' homie

Just because you walk away brother, that don't make you weak

If we take our time to think, maybe we can become something unique

Use the message as food, so the mind can eat

If we change the way we live

Then we won't live for the code of the streets

To Make a Decision

By Juan

The fire in his eyes show the ambition and hunger

While his deathly silence will make you wonder

Never had you seen a young man so calm and poised

When you are used to the youngsters disturbing the peace, making noise

By his demeanor you can tell he's on a mission

A mental one, not a violent one

Man, pay attention

He know that he must do this right

If not then it may cost him his life

To be loyal or to be smart

Loyalty is a must though—it's in his heart

So what's up man, are you going to help us jack this car or what?

You know if you don't go you don't get a cut!

He thought of his struggling mother who had warned him of them

And what it will do to her if something happened to him

Naw man, I can't go. My mom is looking out the window

He lied and left quickly picking up the tempo

A couple hours later at home listening to his radio

Breaking news coming at you live from Club Indigo

Three young men got shot to death trying to jack a car

They tried but they did not get too far

So what are you going to do, they asked

Snapping him out of his vision

No! he said with precise conviction

Because in the end he knew that he made a wise decision!

Always Go Back

By Malik W.

I always go back
I always go back home
I always go back to the hood
I always go back to the love
I always go back to the streets
I try not to go back to the beefs
But I always, always, always go back to that life
My mom tried everything
But I always go back
I want to never go back, never go back, never go back

Poison

By Curtis

See, I met this tall beautiful glass
Filled real nice, and when she comes around
She's cool as ice
When I take in her company
She's the smoothest work of art
My friends tell me she's bad news
And that she might be the death of me
And that she hurt a lot of people
But I'm in love
Nothing can tear us apart
I guess she's my poison

Photo by Tanja Harambasic

CHAPTER 5

TEACH ME

DeCario

As a kid, I felt nervous and ashamed in school. I didn't want the other kids to know I couldn't do the things that everyone else did. I was afraid to get called on because then they'd find out. I just wished I were a ghost. I wanted to go unnoticed. As I got older, I learned to hang with the other kids who didn't want to read or be noticed. We would laugh, joke and act cool instead of paying attention to avoid being called on.

I felt like I couldn't learn to read because I had so much trouble remembering anything. Finally, I just decided it was impossible and that I could not be taught.

In elementary and junior high, I moved to a different school every two or three months because of my mom's addiction. The other kids always seemed to have new clothes, and I was embarrassed that I didn't have those things.

I was in the 9th grade when I was arrested and went to jail. That's where I learned to read, in the Book Club. When I learned to read, it was like, *I can do this!* I realized I actually wanted to learn. It was like the whole world opened up to me when I started reading. I overcame my fear of being looked down upon. Suddenly, I felt more confident.

When I got out of jail, I went to high school and for the first time, I was successful. I moved up several reading levels in just two months. I actually made the dean's list. I remember thinking, *People talk about dean's list all the time. And look at me now! Here I am!* They called me a model student. When I heard that, I felt complete.

I read all the time, now. My favorites are philosophy books. I just got my GED. I have a full-time job and people look up to me. I'm not stopping here though. Next stop, college!

Teach Me

By MarQuell

Teach me and I will learn

Instead of pushin' me away

Show me a way

Instead of calling me dumb

Make me smart

My hand is out

I'm willing to learn

Teach me and I will learn

When will it be my turn?

Like Dr. King, I have a dream

Stop the pain, it burns

Teach me and I will learn

Big Dogs & Cool Cats

By Shakim

He's back! He's back! Who's that?

You know who, the big dog that hangs with those cool cats

Oh yeah, I know him, where's he been?

Freeing his mind through his pad and pen

I just saw him and he spoke words of gloom

He told me to never let my glory walk hand in hand with doom

Said people forget faster than they remember, so remember never to forget

Told me knowledge is like a great wall, so pay attention to every brick

Said success is measured by failure, so learn from their mistakes

He's back! He's back! Who's that?

You know who, the big dog that hangs with those cool cats

D.R.U.M. (Don't Restrain UR Mind!)

By Makkah Ali

Is it because I choose not to think like you

I have a learning disorder?

But in reality the thing you choose to teach and preach

May seem misplaced and out of order

So when it comes to learning your way, it's kinda sorta

Cause my mind is sorta climbing towards the shining border

Enlightenment, enlightenment

Was drifting off in class so I was labeled not bright

Was flushed down the school to prison pipeline

That's just not right

So before I let them place the label on me as being dumb

Because of a misperception of how I look and where I'm from

I tune out the naysayers and march on and march on

To the sound of my own D.R.U.M!

Weapon in my Head

By SD

Most guys' weapon is a gun
But mine is one I can't be separated from
The weapon in my head is so mean
It sounds off like an M-16
When can I learn?
How can I learn?
How much knowledge to earn?
I got mind bullets to burn
Your mind is the worst thing to waste
Feed it all you can like you do your face
Mark my word
Listen to what I said
No weapon is better
Than the weapon in your head

Photo by Peter Broyles

LOVE

Pedro

Puppy love and true love are two different things. When you're young, you think you know, but you don't. I know what true love is now because of the woman in my life. She is my queen. I don't even want to know any other woman now. You just know, right? You just know. I think in life we are lucky if we come across even just one person who is noble, trustworthy and right. And if you're lucky enough to find her, you better hold on and recognize it. Otherwise you'll be regretting it for the rest of your life!

The way they treat you behind bars, it's just so cold. Believe me. There is no love in there! The CO's* are mean and the food is nasty. But out here in the world? Oh man! Love is everywhere. All kinds of love. I mean, when Mama cooks, she puts love in the food, right? So imagine you're sitting in a cell on lockdown all day, your memories start to get to you. You just miss love. Yeah, that's why I wrote about love.

Being in love is absolutely awesome. The best part is that I know she loves me the same. I mean, we do all kind of crazy stuff, that only the two of us understand. I can tell her anything. I can tell her when I'm scared. I wouldn't say that to anyone else. Our chemistry is intertwined like vines. It's like a fairy tale. It was meant to be.

*correctional officers

Yellow to My Blue

By Pedro

Gray is my hue

A sorrow you never knew

A heart without a beat

But love would bring anew

Like when the night precedes the day

So still and mellow

Gives way to the horizon

A magnificent bright yellow

Her love is pure and encrypted

Only she can breathe life into my soul

Days of cold and loneliness

Melt my heart into stone

Yellow to my Blue

Gray is my hue

Skies plagued by showers

Black clouds conceal anew

Gifted with kindness, integrity, bearing and tact

Her courage, love and loyalty are a definite fact

Her smile competes with life's energy source

Her love is a curse whose spell I endorse

Her beauty puts to shame darkness and gloom

One peek at my earth and all the flowers will bloom

Yellow to my Blue

My Special Girl

By Major

Every day is a blessing
But the day God made this girl was special
Because God blessed the world
And the girl changed my world
Without diamonds and pearls
Gave me strength when I was weak
And light when I couldn't see
So when the nights are cold
And she has no one to hold
I hope she knows
I treasure her as if she was gold
 'Cause when times was hard
And I didn't have any friends
God didn't just walk with me
He gave me a friend
That I can love to the end
I know she's praying for me and thinking of me
Because she's my special girl

Nunca Pensé

Por Luis

Jamás imaginé que mi corazón fuera

A sufrir por querer vivir

Siempre pensé que seguir a mi corazón

Sería lo mejor

Muy equivocado que yo estaba

Nunca pensé que esto me pasara

Que perdidamente de ti me enamorara

Y ahora de ti no sé nada

Ahora veo que las promesas, sólo son promesas

Ahora veo que las palabras se las lleva el viento

Ahora veo que el tiempo hace el cambio

"El tiempo todo lo puede"

Nunca pensé que esto a mi me pasara

Jamás hubiera imaginado que la persona

A la cual lo entregué lo mas valioso que tengo

De mi se burlara

Nunca pensé que te perdería de esa manera

Nunca pensé que hasta este punto llegaría

Te sueño, digo tu nombre cuando duermo

Mi corazón no sabe como palpitar

Si tú no estás aqui conmigo

Estoy vivo pero mi corazón extraña tu calor

En este invierno si no me muero de frío

Me muero de tristeza

Nunca pensé que hasta este punto llegar

I Never Thought

By Luis

I never imagined that my heart
Would suffer for wanting to live
I always thought that following my heart
Would be best
How wrong I was
I never thought this would happen to me
How hopelessly in love with you I'd be
And now I know nothing of you
Now I see that the promises are only promises
Now I see that the words are gone with the wind
Now I see that time changes
"Time changes all that it can"
I never thought this would happen to me
I never could have imagined that the person
To whom I gave the most valuable thing I have
Would laugh at me
I never thought I would lose you this way
I never thought it would come to this
I dream of you, I say your name in my sleep
My heart doesn't know how to beat
If you aren't here with me
I am alive but my heart misses your heat
In this winter if I don't die of cold
I will die of sadness
I never thought it would come to this

Without You

By Deante

Without you I am like…
A lamp with no light, a heart with no blood
A body with no soul, a baby with no love
A car with no gas, a skull with no brain
A gun with no bullets, a lighter with no flames
A beach with no water, a plane with no pilot
The sky with no sun, a child with no guidance
A bird with no wings, a snake with no head
A fish with no fin, a kangaroo with no legs
A kid with no toys, a head with no ears
A man with no conscience, eyes with no tears
A hand with no fingers, a house with no roof
Salt with no pepper, a spoon with no soup
Legs with no feet, paper with no pen
A bike with no wheels, a boy with no friend
Goals with no plans, a plate with no food
Lost and so empty, I'm useless without you

Mysterious Woman

By Vincent

From a girl to woman
I truly love and care about
I'm sorry I left out of her life
It wasn't my intention to leave
I promise myself to come back and do better
And make her smile every day
It's been a long time
And it hurts me every day
I get through my days in prison
By the special memories we share
Now she all grown up
Looking beautiful
With two pretty young daughters
I never got the chance to hold

Belonging to Love

By Yester

I want to belong to something
To something positive
I want to belong to the community that rejected me
To the streets that I can't walk through now
But I'm going to hit them one day
And I know I belong to my family
To something special in their hearts
To something that is never going to go away
To something that's never gonna change
That's what I belong to
I belong to love

Photo by Peter Broyles

PAIN

David

When I was little, I lived with my mother. I always wondered about my father, but nobody, not my mom, or my aunts would ever tell me where he was. Finally, my grandmother said, "Don't tell nobody this David, but your dad is locked up. He got 32 years to life." Oh man, that hurt.

My first experience with emotional pain as an adult though was when I was 19 years old and my mother passed. It was like someone dropped a ton of bricks on me. It was even worse because I was locked up. It was a shock. It's funny because the word spread in prison and dudes would turn up giving me their canteen and saying, "It's gonna be aiight." But you can't say, "It's gonna be aiight." Some dudes would kill themselves over their mother passing. Nobody can understand it if it hasn't happened to them. That was pain for real!

Since then, the pain I've felt has all been my own fault, because I keep going in and out of prison. I know I can do good things and keep from getting locked up. I know it, and yet some how, some way, the devil gets the best of me. I'm 26 now and I been getting locked up since I was 13. That's half my life! And to think of all of the positive I could have been doing during that time? The regret. That's what hurts me most.

The pain is always going to be layin' around me. It's there because I wish I never got locked up. But you never know how something good may come out of pain. Maybe one day I might be able to help someone else going through something similar. Wisdom comes from pain. Being free now, staying focused, I feel like I know I can do better and I know I can stay out of jail.

I know this: Tryin' isn't enough. I could always be quick to be bad. Now I just gotta be quick to be good.

When I wrote this poem, "Stressin'," I was really hurting. Writing is such a relief though. Especially when you locked up. Because even if nobody else gonna listen to you, that paper will! And that pencil will!

Stressin'

By David

Day and night I'm stressin'
Every day I strive to do good
But I see no progression
But why it gotta be me?
Why it gotta be D.A.V.I.D.?
And it's more people like me
So when I'm really stressin'
I drop to the ground and work out
But my mind is cloudy so that don't work out
Runnin' thoughts is what's in my cognitive
I might do negative but I still think positive
I know there's light at the end of the tunnel
So in the mean time I'ma twist up this loud and fronto
And feel how it go away
It's not forever but for a day
But once back sober stress really sinks in deeper
And she's a creeper you don't want to meet her
And I hope you don't cross her
Runnin' away thinkin' that you lost her
But you haven't
Because that's what you go through in life
And we still stress even when we do right
Even though I got this off my chest
Right now I'm stressin'

Why Is My Heart So Cold?

By Tavon

Why is my heart so cold?

Is it 'cause the way the wind blows?

Is it the way the rain pours?

The reason that I can't feel no more

Or is it 'cause my mother wasn't there?

Or that I never saw my father and he don't care?

Or is it 'cause of these streets?

My only friends getting murdered 'cause of beef

My only blood getting taken away from me

They say there's a lot good and warm in this world

Seems like more bad and cold if you ask me

Good spirits I do not enter

Summer outside but inside me it's winter

Good times I seem to not remember

Cold like the first winter chill in December

Why is my heart so cold? I still don't know

But as I live on, the coldness in my heart continues to grow

God?

By Darrell

If you there, God, and you can hear, God
Send me to hell, yeah, I'm prepared, God
Give me a slow death, I want the chair, God

You ain't a fair God, you don't care, God
If you can hear, God, then why ain't you here, God
You a rare God, 'cause you never there, God
When I'm sad, God, you become a glad God
You never satisfied even when I give you everything I have, God

Where's my dad, God? Are you my dad, God?
'Cause if you are, I don't wanna follow in your path, God
And if I'm your work of art, then you did a bad job

Your Son failed God, how could you let him take them nails, God?
He was impaled, God, I know you heard him yell God
I guess it's all good, but where's the Holy Grail, God?

Answer the question, God, am I your self-reflection, God?
Do you rock dreads, an earring, and a bright shiny necklace, God?
Is that even me, God? Then tell me who you see, God
'Cause before I get back on my knees, God, I'd rather rest in peace, God

My good deeds, God? What good deeds, God?
How could I be humble to a million enemies, God?
What is life, God? WHAT IS LIFE, GOD?!
Never mind, just tell me why it comes with a price, God

You see my mom, God? That's your wife, God
Watch her for me please, be her lifeguard
I just hope that she believes in the right God

What's wrong, God? Are you alright, God?

The questions I never heard you ask your child on these cold nights, God

Peace

By Rafael

You ever went through something so painful
You'd rather sleep than be awake?
I'm not talking about physical pain, but mental pain
There's more at stake!
When I sleep
It's so pleasant, I don't want to wake
When I'm woke
It's so painful, I can't think straight!
I don't know what to do
I just want to go home
I just want peace
Just want to be left alone
When I sleep
I'm free of this madness that's going on
When I sleep
I'm free with my family
I don't want to wake
Is that wrong?

Feel My Pain

By Alvin

Feel my pain stuck in the game

Trying to play it different ways

But the results always the same

Being stereotyped by what's on paper

Before I get to speak

Employers scared to look in my eyes

Because they might get weak

And see that I am striving

And searching for a better life

So they hold their heads down

And read my background

And always think twice

What am I to do with three mouths to feed?

Turn back to what I was raised around

And then I'm considered to be wrong

Am I wrong for trying to survive?

Or am I wrong for the many lives I jeopardized?

No one sees the struggle

They only see the trouble

Now I'm labeled a menace to society

And all my charges are doubled

Everyone in the world is different

But our struggles are all the same

So I know there are many different versions

To "feel my pain"

Ascend

By Darrell

My worries make me upset
And my toils make me bitter
My heart always misleads me
But my blood pumps quicker
My soul has been drowned
And my wings have been clipped
I was once a glorious angel
But now I roam the devil's pit
Full of transgressions
Violence quenches my thirst
I know no one can find me
But I still seek to be searched
I bow my head in shame
As chains hold me to the ground
There are others just like me
But I can't blend in with the crowd
Boils grow all over my body
As I get slashed with a whip
Pain gets lost in memory
As my bones become content
Tears turn into ashes
Skin turns into dust
But the light beckons for my attention
As God lifts me up
Dust turns into skin
Ashes into tears
My wings grow twice as big
As my soul reappears
As I ascend into the light
I take one last look at hell
I still know my battle awaits me
But with God I can never fail

Emotion

By SD

Sometimes I wish I was heartless

So I wouldn't care

Use a black hole to replace the red muscle

So I won't fear when you ain't there

And I won't have to struggle

I need the potion for no emotion

Or to put them in a bottle to go with the ocean

Don't want to be happy—I'll end up sad

Don't want to feel all right—I'll end up mad

Don't want them—kick them out the door

What the H-E-Double-Hockey-Sticks

I need emotion for?

Dreams

By Juwan

Why have dreams

If dreams don't come true

I don't have dreams

I have nightmares

My Unspoken Words

By Antwan

Pain, grief, trauma is what my words endure
My life, my struggle, my mind is scorned
This can't be real! Why? I squeal
They took my brother's life by the power of the steel
I see rage, I feel in a daze, revenge is the only deal
How am I supposed to feel?
My nieces n' nephews have to go fatherless by the act of a coward
And where was I?
In a cell watching my life fly by
Can't even be there for my mother
Hold her while she cry
No funeral, no min's
The Feds didn't even let me tell my brothers bye
Now the only time I can talk to my brothers
Is when I look to the sky
My mother told me to stay strong n' move on
I am her baby boy, the last out of four!
It's all up to me
I can turn it up when I hit the streets
Or be there for the family
Cause now is the time they really need me
So I got to be a man n' let God play his hand
The kids got to eat, they need somewhere to sleep
So I got to think about them before I go chasing that beef
My mind is on a mission
My heart is dealing with some issues
My actions is saying forget you
And my words is always against you
I need to change, I think I need help
But who can I talk to
When I'm never goin' to open up
I have a whole lot of worries and a lot more questions
These are the words of my unspoken destiny

Photo by Peter Broyles

THE ROCKY ROAD

Calvin

I was 16 when a woman identified me as the person who carjacked her. I was arrested and sentenced to 15 years. I felt like my whole future was snatched from me. I felt hopeless. I wouldn't have the opportunity to finish high school. I'd never go to my prom. I wouldn't be going to college, which was all I wanted to do. I felt like it was taken from me.

I remember when my motion for a new trial was denied. I couldn't believe it. It all seemed bleak for me. I was pressing my bunk. That's what they call it when you just lay back because there's nothing to do but lay back. I felt like it was going to be a very long while 'til I got my freedom. There was one more chance for the judge to reconsider. He denied it again. My world came crashing down.

I know it sounds crazy, but those are the moments that made me who I am today. Dealing with the mental challenges of being incarcerated -- being away from my family -- it helped me become strong. Most importantly, I learned how to be patient. I could have given up and taken it out on others. A lot of people get bitter instead of better. The way you get treated in prison, I can testify, it would be easy to get bitter.

It's just so important to persevere. Even when you feel hopeless, you have to take advantage of every opportunity to read, write and get your education. When I was in prison I kept myself occupied spiritually and intellectually. It allowed me to get through the times I felt depressed.

I always knew I was different. This challenge made me realize who I really am. While I was locked up, I built a relationship with my Creator. The experience secured my self-esteem and confidence. I am comfortable in my own skin. I've always been different, but I just didn't know how to embrace it in a positive way.

Now I feel so great about my life. I see things coming to fruition, step by step. I am touching lives and that's what matters in the long run.

My story is bittersweet. Bitter at first, sweet at the end.

Calvin's initial conviction was overturned.
In 2013, he was released after serving six and a half years in prison.

Rocky Road

By AG

As I travel this rocky road

Obstacles await me I once was told

So I humble myself in order to prepare

And not fall victim to meaningless despair

In the back of my mind streets calling my name

Yelling/screaming, jail doing the same

I hold my head up and continue my walk

Consumed with the thought

That days will get better

Is this frivolous talk?

It's a daily struggle when wearing my shoes

Statistically speaking, I'm destined to lose

Either live with the odds or open my eyes

It's me who controls my own demise

The strong will progress

The weak will fold

Are you bold enough

To travel this rocky road?

Don't Listen to Them

By Talib

In this world where negativity plays a role in your life

Keep your focus on the things that's good

When someone approaches you with words that are not nice

If you have an ambition to go after a goal

That you think you can achieve

Set your goal and you must believe

Keep your mind positive because you are what you think

And know that you can leave a legacy

That can stain like a pen when it releases ink

They say a positive mind is contagious

So spread the disease

You can become whatever you want to be

All you have to do is believe

What Comes Next

By Paulo

As you read these words
You wonder what is to come next
My story unfolds in an unpredictable fashion
That's right
I was born in one country, but raised in another
I had two parents, but I sided with one
As a child, I was raised to attend school and help out at home
In my adolescence, I found the streets and friends entertaining
Finally, by the age of 17 handcuffs were slapped to my wrists
No home, friends, nor streets to run to
But the story does not end like this
Years later, I sat in the front row of my graduating class
Not far apart, I worked full-time teaching others
Around the corner, I found myself being slammed against a wall
Again, I was handcuffed
And this time I was placed in a box
From here, I was led on a long ride up to a mountain
Fences were long gone
High cement walls and high towers became my new home
Today, seven years later, I sit on my bed
Pondering how my life unfolded since my birth

The Game Plan

By Michael

Success on my mind
You should think tha same and I ain't playin' no games
I gotta big ol' brain
That could learn some thangs
I'ma go real far 'cause I was born a star
I'ma touch tha moon and I'ma walk on Mars
Give honor to God
Be who I am
Take care of tha fam
Thinkin' life is a game, y'all playin'
Man I'm just sayin'
Young brova you should start wit' a plan
Start wit' a dream
Den when you finish dat
Young brova, you should form you a team
But not any team
Form you a squad that's on the same means with a dream
Success is tha dream
Get it on your mind and you could obtain anything
I'm a real brova
Southeast DC where I'm from
Where I wasn't taught to run
I was taught to go hard brova
And I don't need a gun
Nah, I don't need a gun
I'ma make it to tha top and when I get there I'm not done
I ain't doin' dis for fun
I'm doin' dis for me, my fam and my brovas in tha slums
Real life level one
Education is the key
Plan A don't work, you got B
Summin' dat my momma told me
Son, I want chu be betta than me
So, I'ma live to my potential
Betta' know dat I got tha credentials
You playin' wit' them guns
Sooner or later boy
Your momma gon' miss you

El Camino

Por Luis

El camino ese es el que tengo que seguir. Muchas dicen que este camino está lleno de peligros, en este camino no hay amigos ni luz que ilumine por dónde caminas.

El camino está lleno de obstáculos que con tu vida pueden terminar. En este camino tu corazón será roto y tu felicidad pueden robar, tus ojos con lágrimas se llenarán.

El camino es largo, muchos no alcanzan a llegar y con tu vida lo tienen que pagar. El corazón se te llenará de soledad y vivirás experiencias que nunca querrás repetir.

El camino tú lo creas y si te equivocas con tu vida lo pagaras, si no alcanzas a llegar, la cena de los cuervos serás en este camino sin que lo sepas eres la presa de la maldad.

En el camino hay muchos que no te darán la mano, piedras somos y en el camino andamos, muchos dicen que sólo con golpes avanzamos, somos piedras y la vida a veces con patadas nos usen seguir un camino en el cual tus sentimientos no cuentan.

El camino está lleno de sueños rotos. En este camino se han perdido muchas sonrisas a que se han vivido años de luz. Historias más duras de contar y el que las escucha con lágrimas en los ojos vivirá.

El camino no tiene salida y si no sabes ver más allá de camino de tu alma se apoderara, esta camino está marcado por el sufrimiento de aquellos que con sus vidas han pagado.

El camino está lleno de peligros que tu corazón envenena y a tu felicidad amenazan, en el camino muchos han perdido la fe, aquí no hay amigos sino los hay ellos representan el peligro.

El camino es una trampa,solo te sufrirás en el camino no hay amor ni sentimientos aquí la esperanza se la lleva el viento aquí los golpes te usan avanzar y tu corazón se alimenta con lágrimas llenas de soledad

The Road

By Luis

This road is the one I have to follow. Many say it's full of danger. On this road there are no friends, nor light to show the way.

This road is full of obstacles that can end your life. On this road your heart will be broken and your happiness can be stolen. Tears will fill your eyes.

This road is long, many don't make it, and you pay with your life. Your heart will fill with loneliness, and you'll live through things you never want to repeat.

You create the road and if you're wrong you'll pay with your life. If you don't make it, you'll be a feast for the crows on this road without knowing that you're food for evil.

On the road there are many that won't give you their hand. We are stones and on the road we walk, many say that you only advance with blows. We are stones and at times life kicks us to keep on the road where your feelings don't matter.

The road is full of broken dreams. On this road many smiles that have lived in light for years have been lost. He who hears the stories most difficult to tell with tears in their eyes will live.

The road has no exit and if you don't know to look ahead your soul will be overpowered. This road is marked by the suffering of those who paid with their lives.

The road is full of dangers that will poison your heart and threaten your happiness. On this road many have lost their faith. Here there are no friends, only those who represent danger.

The road is a trick and you will only suffer on the road. There is no love nor feelings here, where the wind carries the hope and the violence uses you to advance and your heart feeds on tears full of loneliness.

Free Mindz Rap

By Raymond

Now I know what it's like to have a Free Mind

I was lost, blindfolded, to see crime

One day I'm on the street, to see shine

Next day I'm in the pen, to see time

The judge told me he gave me a second chance

This is the longest I have ever been in the slam

Free Mindz is family, family for what I stand

The more that I grow, the more I'm becoming a man

You might as well move forward and concentrate

I still have a date with the world, I'm not late

You can get around the bad, just navigate

You can still change your life, so why wait?

Reading and writing is all that I have

Making good judgment is creating a path

You should hurry up and change all you can

Time is ticking, you do the math

Reentry

By Bennett

Reentry is like coming out the womb for the second time

It's a new beginning

Don't really know where to start

When it come to finding a job

Or just getting my life together

I got to put some people and things behind me to move forward

These streets a beast

It's like a chess game

I'm the king that controls my army

I got to make my next move my best move

Got to pay attention and never snooze

'Cause in this game you will lose

To a world that is cruel

So it's all about how I move

Got to stay on my A game at all times

Watch the company I keep

Or it will put me back in a place

Where I don't want to be

It's about change

Going Where?

By Kenny

Where am I goin'?

I'm still tryna figure out

Like slaves from way back

I feel I need to make it out

With a lil' motivation and a lil' push on

I got all I need to find out where I'm goin'

I'ma keep it moving forward

Like slaves headin' north I'm not stoppin'

Until I get where I'm goin'

Upstream

By Rafael

Upstream, upstream
I have to make it upstream!
The current is so strong
I don't know if I can make it
I've been swimming so long
I don't know how much longer my body can take it
Mentally and physically weakened
Upstream, upstream, can I make it?
I just want to be at peace
I just want to rest
Can I make it up the stream
Where there's freedom and no distress?
Sometimes I just want to stop
And just go with the flow
I can drown to a watery tomb or float to freedom
Who will ever know?
I close my eyes as I relax
And pray for the better
Don't give up, you're almost there
Don't give up!
My family and friends believe
They cheer me on!
I open my eyes and jolt forward
And push and push and push!
Upstream, upstream
I will be free
I will make it up stream!
Tough situations only last for a minute
But tough people last forever
I am forever tough
And this stream is a little obstacle
And I will hold together
Upstream, upstream
I will make it and be free forever!

Turn on the Lights

By Thomas

Looking for that star in the sky
Reaching for my dreams
Wishing to be the best at what I do
Motivating me with a twinkle of light
In a world of haters
Turn on my light brighter
So my people, my family and friends
Can see me shine bright in a life of hell
Where I beat the devil
By accomplishing my dreams
Even though people told me
I wouldn't be anything
I proved them wrong
So turn up the lights so that we can all
Shine bright like diamonds in that sky
Freeing us to be all that we can be
Our kids, our future, our friends, our families
Turn them up so that we can all see them
Shining bright

CHAPTER 9

Photo by Peter Broyles

DREAMIN' OF FREEDOM

Andre

I was behind bars for 12 years. When I got sentenced at the age of 16, I felt like everything I knew just wasn't no more. Like I lost everything.

Cement and metal. Metal and cement. A person can't fathom what that's like. I felt like I was fighting time. Me and time was going at it. But time moved the way it wanted, not the way I wanted.

Finding out I'd lost my mom was the worst. She died while I was in prison. My family told me on the phone. I didn't get to go to the funeral. I just broke down. Being strong wasn't an option.

I was on solitary confinement for 16 months. I didn't see nobody. I worked out, I made prayer, I read books and I wrote. I daydreamed all of the time about what I was missing. Man, I even dreamed about raking the yard. But you know what I missed most of all? Helping someone. Like, just helping an old lady carry her bags. I missed helping anyone period.

I woke up every single day wondering, *Man, is this real?* Even after 10 years. But I'm glad that I felt that way. Being incarcerated is nothing a person should get used to. I never did.

The day that I was released, oh man! I was trying to see everything and everyone. I just watched people. What they wore, the way they walked and talked and interacted. I was just taking it all in. I felt like everyone was watching me too. Like I looked different, somehow. But that felt good. I was finally free where people could see me. Now I feel like I can tap that potential button. I've got all this potential inside of me, and I can finally put it to use.

Freedom tastes like this cereal I'm eating right now. Sweet, healthy, and all mine! This is the first time I've had Fruity Pebbles in almost 13 years.

The Unexpected

By Paulo

The doors open and I am escorted in

Wearing an oversized orange jumpsuit

I glance around and find myself being stared at

The air circulating in the room

Brings goose bumps to my skin

I just want to run away

I want to hide

And erase the moment

The judge calls out my name

Within minutes, my future is called out

I am left speechless

Escorted out, I struggle to move my legs

My knees want to give up on me

I cannot hold myself together

I am still adding the numbers

Title 16*

By Khyree

The title I was given does not make me a champion
Nor would I brag or boast about it
Under 18 down in the jail
And now all of a sudden DC does not give bail
Never thought I'd be here
Writing this poem
Or seeing my mother through a TV screen
Talking through a phone
I'm considered a minor
But in an adult environment
The title I received
Instead of a championship belt
Is shackles and handcuffs

**Title 16 refers to the DC law that allows juveniles to be charged and
incarcerated as adults in adult facilities for certain offenses*

I Used To

By Donald

I used to hold my head up high
Until the comments from CO's*
And big words from courtrooms
Knocked me down
I used to see the beauty in the sky
Until the horrific and bloody scenery
Stained my eyes
I used to live life without a care
Until I saw peoples' feelings get hurt with just a stare
Missing the times when I could feel happy
Without caution, yeah, I used to be there
I used to take things for granted
Now I miss and long for everything I had
I used to do what I wanted, didn't need luck
Can't wait for my next poem when I'll write…
"I used to be locked up"

correctional officers

Looking Out My Cell Window

By Malik

Looking out my window, I see the sky

Envision me working on the cloud next to nine

Staring at the sun, I see to its core

The fire that burns around it is like a boy

A flame that is angry, pained and sad

Waiting to burn, since the day it was born

Looking out my window, I see the moon

Jumping on the stars, I am not that far

From the cool nice night that a boy wishes he had

He's bright like the moon, but small as Pluto

He runs through the night on a mission

He jumps over the broom, but is stuck with bad luck

Because he ran into a room, with no way out

Now the only thing he can do

Is watch the days and the nights fly past

Like a bird speeding past on a sunny day

Vision over

Lights out

Bedtime…

18 to 42

By CM

See, ONE mistake changed my life
In numerous ways
And I'm talking for TWO decades
Not the "soon to be" days
Who would've thought that THREE seconds
Could mean so many years?
Never imagined my TWO eyes crying
So many tears
With ONE life to live
And a MILLION dreams subdued
The front prison gates
Is where my childhood concludes
Pleaded to TWENTY-FOUR years
And that's just something I gotta do
But I'll be ready to explore the world
On the year I turn FORTY-TWO

Time

By Brandon

I sit back and think

Every day all I ever hear is

Time to wake up!

At 2:30

Time to eat!

At 4:30

Time to come out!

At 9:30

Your time is up!

Now it's count time

Why do I have to be counted?

I want to be counted as a good person

Not as an inmate

All I can think of is time

I may be locked up with time

But my name is free as can be

I Couldn't Win

By LA

Like a moth captured, I remain confined

Those looking in are unable to set me free

My freedom's revoked, when I speak I choke

I try to talk, but my words simply flee

My once beautiful wings are becoming brittle

My fragile body's becoming sore

The windows to my soul are clouded with despair

My gentle heart is now torn

I look for a helping hand

No one to rescue me from my stress

I am claustrophobic in this jar

Lack of ventilation's making me lose my breath

I'm slowly losing my strength

By tomorrow I'll be dead and gone

After years of fighting a battle I couldn't win

The Sunset

By Tyrell

When I see the sunset from my cell
Sometimes I want to cry
Then I think about peace
And then I see
Things are gonna get much better
The sunset makes me feel comforted
And it calms me down
Before I go to sleep
The sunset

Painter

By Yester

Painter, change the color of my painting
Give it a little bit of color 'cause it's dark
Put some sky blue so I can have a taste of liberty
Erase these walls that hold me down
And add some wings to me
To fly far away from my captivity
'Cause my daily living is sad and full of darkness
And many rain clouds gather around me
Leaving me wet with pain and cold in my soul
Paint a brilliant sun in my life so I can get dry
Because I've been trying to get dry with this cold breeze
But instead of getting dry, I get more cold
Add the word home in my road
And the word family in my future
And I'll be grateful the rest of my entire life

No Mail

By Deante

I'm alone, held captive, confined within these walls

Listening to, *Mail time!* every time the guard calls

I haven't received a letter yet and I know nothing going to change

But still I rush to the front of the line, hoping he calls my name

Inmates' names are being called, and I'm watching smiles appear

But Deante is a name I never hear

Quickly I turn away, on the verge of tears

Wondering why no one wrote me, do they even know I'm here?

Moving quickly, I got back to my cell, ready to cry myself to sleep

Praying that I'll receive a letter

Days turn into weeks and weeks turn into months

I listen, listen, and listen but don't hear my name once

Still haven't received a letter yet and I know nothing going to change

So I'm done listening to mail call, they're never going to call my name

On Friday the 13th, my cellmate tells me, *Today's your lucky day*

Ten minutes later, *Deante you have mail*, is what the guards say

I open the letter, eager to read it, smiling from ear to ear

But when I open the envelope and see indictment papers, my smile disappears

Now it seems for a long time, I'ma be stuck in a cell

Held captive, all alone, still waiting on my mail

Locked Up

By Jonas

All I've got are my dreams
All I've got are my visions
Trying to calculate ways to execute my own missions
Coming from a low place where stackin' bread was the issue
But if you get shot today, ain't nobody gonna miss you
My deep past in contrast to the things that I've learned
Got me focused on all of the strong bridges I've burned
Incarcerated, I'm packin'—the tool I'm lackin' is patience
I need to slow it on down, instead I'm actin' all anxious
Every day is a war—I'm fighting for self-preservation
In hopes that one day it'll be the air of freedom I'm tastin'
Chasin' dreams, escaping reality when I can
All I've got is my pride—I will remain a man
Educating myself, slowly evicting my ignorance
If I've got a big problem, I break it down and I figure it
This here life is a lesson, a blessin' given from God
If I stumble and fall, I pick it up and restart
The library, my sanctuary with thousands of books
I keep reading when I'm receiving these venomous looks
From characters that think it's a game and ain't realized
I'm a man, there's no doubt when you look in these eyes
I rise to the test when cowards puff up their chest
Devour one and I'm sending a message to all of the rest
Avoiding conflicts ain't easy for convicts
When paranoia and stress is what causes this nonsense
The soul of a prison is power and control
I'm telling you people, it grows so old
Simply the story is told, bold, with truth as its essence
I'm only speakin' my truth but I hope you're feelin' my message

Wildfire

By Mike

Good morning, Gorgeous
The wind blows across my face to reply back
Last night I was tossing, turning and dreaming
Of the day we would be back in each other's life
Stressful days and sleepless nights
Sometimes me and Slim would sit up late night
Reminiscing how we'd yet again ruined our life
Sometimes it's like a wild fire
You think you have it put out and *Boom*! You lose control
How could I risk losing you again?
Anything can come true
I'm lucky to be able to reunite with you
I know guys that can only talk about good times they had with you
I don't get mad, only ponder
How I'll enjoy you this time around
FREEDOM! FREEDOM! FREEDOM! FREEDOM!
I guess you're gone now, so until our next date

Purple and Gold Passion

By David

Purple and gold skies

Magnificent

As my heart yearns for more

I close my eyes

Collect my thoughts

Think about my passion for living

Am I living?

Through several windows and fences

I see purple and gold skies

My passion

Zoom

By Ahmad

I'd like to fly
Fly away from here
To a place where my mind can be fresh and clear
I never pictured incarceration so young
So many missed opportunities
My songs unsung
I often think of myself as polished with potential
Is it that others cannot see me in the same light?
Or is it so many years of wrongdoing
Allows my subconscious to whisper it's right?
Oh, how I wish I could take flight
My engine would roar in the late night
And sleepless souls would be enlightened
Dark skies I would brighten
Destroy unjust indictments
Silence the sirens of abusive authority
Tell me if the mother's in the ho house
Then where would the daughter be?
If the father's in the jailhouse then where is the son?
In federal prison Title Sixteen'd*
With dreams and steps to greatness that never begun
I'd like to fly away from here
To a place where my mind can be so very fresh and clear
George Zimmerman gunned down Trayvon Martin
What kind of justice is this?
Surely not the type Old Abe or Dr. King would permit
A young soul cries where darkness would conceal his lonely one tear
Zoom…
I'd sure like to fly away from here…

Title 16 refers to the DC law that allows juveniles to be charged and incarcerated as adults in adult facilities for certain offenses

Outside Four Walls

By Eddie

Life outside four walls

Not guilty!

On all 21 counts

We all get blessings

That are deserved in some way

People who know this feeling are few

Some still can't explain

How it really feels

To do what you want

When you want

How you want

7/21/12

I'm free from staring at four walls!

After being told what to do

For three and a half years

No probation

No judge

I am free, free, free!

I inhale

Then exhale

The last breath of jail

Headed Home

By Kevin B.

I'm headed home

I'm almost there

I'm on my way

Headed up the stairs

To what I like best

A mother, a brother, a girl and our daughter

I am going to spoil her

I'm headed home to live life

Maybe even fly a kite

Or even teach my daughter

How to ride a bike

I'm headed home

My family won't even pick up the phone

Headed home with no ride

Or cab to drive

But I'm glad the jail gave me bus tokens

That means nobody's car had to get stolen

I'm headed home

I'm not cold or alone

I'm just glad that I'm home

Headed home

THEY

By DeAngelo

THEY say I'm only a kid

So why did *THEY* sentence me as a man?

THEY threw me away for 10 years

And my young mind never understood what *THEY* were saying

THEY never once tried to take my hand

All *THEY* did was try to make me tell on the next young man

THEY was the ones who told me I needed to be good and do right

But *THEY* was the ones I went to and asked for a job and *THEY* took flight

So to this day, *THEY* are the ones I stand up to and fight

Because someone has to be around that been through these things in life

To give that next young man a voice and a shining light

And I will do so with all my might

Cold Hours and Sunlight

By PM

There was a time when days and nights were the same

Didn't make any difference so I pretended to play a game

If a there was light then I had to wait for the night

Tick-tock, Tick-tock, Tick-tock

And if it was dark I had to wait for the light

It went on and on for days so I got tired and stopped counting

But in my mind the numbers always followed like a lurking shadow

At that moment my life felt...(Umm what's that word?)...oh yeah...
really...hollow

I looked at the walls and even without eyes it stared right at me

So I stared at it, mugged at it and punched at it...felt so apoplectic

No matter what...there was so much pain just to be me

Now I look back at the past and see and tell myself it is all behind me

And now every day I tell myself it feels amazing just to be free

Finally Free

By Calvin

My mind constantly racing, as I'm walking out of those gates

I stop and pause, not knowing my fate

What's next? Am I really ready?

Some things that weigh upon my conscience so heavy

But the sweet taste of freedom overlaps my concerns

Because it's something for so long that I yearned

And aside from that, beneficial lessons I learned

That shaped and molded my character, as I waited my turn

A picture painted so vivid, now clearer I see

A new beginning for me, now that I'm finally free

CHAPTER 10

Photo by Peter Broyles

RIP

Phil

I met Jay when I was 11. Me and his little brother were friends and you know how that is. All of us became thick as thieves. Our relationship was like brothers. Jay was the oldest of all of us, so we looked up to him.

Jay and I were together when I found out another one of our other closest friends, Charlie, was killed. I was 15 and it was the first time I'd lost someone to the streets. By then, most people have lost two of three of their friends. But now I realize, 15? That's a young age to die. Jay and I just cried together. A year later, I got locked up for ten years.

I remember it was May 14th last year, just a few months before I would be going home from prison. A guy from DC told me, "You need to call home. I just got a feelin' somebody died." He didn't know, but I called my Mom and she asked if I was sitting down. Then she told me Jay got killed. Ah man, it hurt. It hurt real bad.

That was my man! It's crazy because Jay had been locked up too, and he just wrote me that he was home. I ain't never got to talk to him. Jay was funny. He was loving and generous too. I look back at it now, and from the age of 16, I only knew Jay through letters and phone calls. You go missing from each other for that long, you gotta get to know each other all over again. I never got to know him as an adult.

When I hung up, I broke down right there on the block. My whole thought process changed in an instant. My thoughts went to revenge. For three weeks I was messed up and I couldn't think of nothing else but getting revenge for Jay. Then one day, my friend told me, "You just did ten years. You can't go and give it all back now!" Suddenly, it clicked. Jay's the one who told me that we had to do things differently. He's the one who told me to be positive. It was so hard though because all this time, I was just waiting to get out there with Jay and make it together. And he was out there by himself without me, and he couldn't do it alone.

Expressing myself with a pen and paper and writing poems helped me to let go of the anger about Jay's death. I go and see his family and spend time with his niece and nephew. I took them skating. I can't look at Jay's obituary though. I still can't do it.

All He Wanted

By Phil

All he wanted was a better way

He told me to focus on Ma Dukes and Lil' Bro'

All he wanted was to be there for me

He told me, *Big Boy, come out and live!*

All he wanted was to be there for his niece and nephew, his world

He told me, *Brah, it's hard but I'm maintaining*

All he wanted was a person to hear him out

In the end, he lost it all

Rest In Peace, Jermaine "Jay" Dews

Gone but never forgotten

Pain to Power

By Alonzo

I was 14 when I watched Ky die

When I seen him fall back and close his eyes

I didn't want to believe he was dying

So I ain't cry

I just talked to my boy like he was alive

I felt as if I lost part of me

As if part of me died

It hurt so badly, I wanted to lie beside him in a casket

And go with him

Some people would have sworn I was a zombie

Walking thru the hood

But I took the pain and turned it into poems

Now I feel as if he's living in me

As if I'm the reincarnation of him

Now I am totally different

Because his legacy lives on through me

What's Your Number?

By MC

I know five people who been shot
All five of them died
It doesn't surprise me
Stuff just be happening
Too many beefs going on
For real, for real?
There's no reason
This stuff is happening for no reason at all
My friend got killed right in front of me when I was 15
His name was Dontae
I don't even know what happened
We was in the hallway cooling
We didn't even know this guy
He came in and BAM! BAM!
The noise was so loud, I blacked out
When I came to, everyone was just yelling
I looked at Dontae and he was on the ground
I figured he'd blacked out too
I thought the sound was just too loud for his ears
He still had his hands in his Helly Hansen jacket
But then they rolled him over on his side
And he started to choke
Blood just started pouring out of his mouth
After that I knew
After that everything changed
Dontae?
He was a straight A student
He wouldn't hurt a fly
He was respectful to his parents
And funny?
That's what I liked the most about him
He was so funny!
His parents, they were so mad
The police did catch the guy who did it
I just don't even know
I don't have any idea
What we can do to make the violence stop
I ain't gonna lie
I can't come up with anything

I Miss

By Tobias

I miss my mother

On special days

And special nights

I miss all the cuss outs

All the arguments

And all the fights

I miss the great times and the bad

I miss the happy times and the sad

I know I wasn't the best son

I just want you to know I love you, Ma!

Rest in peace to the best mother in the world.

Tyree (Before the Sword)

By Antwon

Dedicated to Tyree, a Free Minds member who lost his life to gun violence on November 8, 2013

What good is a reputation

If it demands the lives of millions of young black men and women to attain it?

Surely, we have forgotten that our blood is sacred

And our youthfulness is pure

At least it was before we picked up the sword

What is the sword?

The sword is drugs, violence, money, and guns

These are the things that hold more weight in our heart than love

Maybe the truth is we are our own worst enemies

We are so concerned with people's general opinions

When half of young men are ignorant

I mean, will it kill us to look in the mirror?

Or are we as scared of our own reflection

As a groundhog is of its own shadow?

Matter of fact, I want you to close your eyes

And imagine that you are a working 25 year-old young man

You have a seven year-old son

Who is the spitting image of you

And loves his Daddy dearly

For once in your life

Smile at the fact that you are trying to better yourself

Now, open your eyes

Only to see a bloody shirt as screams echo through the air

This was Tyree (before the sword)

Memories

By Trey

What happens when memories are all you have left?
No pictures, letters, or cards…just memories
Sooner or later our memory starts to fade
So do you play the images back constantly?
Or just hold on for as long as you can?
My memories play like a movie
And always start early in my childhood
She's there giving me love
What would happen if she left and didn't come back?
I pause on my early adolescent days
At the age where I'm old enough
To roam the neighborhood
And be embarrassed by her showing love in public
Would I act differently
Knowing I need her loving more than ever?
Fast forward to my high school years
I started singing in a go-go band
She's too old for this crowd and music
But she's still my #1 fan
So what's a star when his most important fan is missing?
The last of my memories hurt the most
I want to make them fuzzy
But they become more vivid than the others
Our last conversation continues to play in my sleep
And when I wake, there's dried tears on my cheeks
Is it possible for your heart to break
In more pieces than it's made of?
So what do you do
When memories are all you have left?
You cherish them and be thankful
You were able to make them

Photo by Renee Billingslea

A PENCIL IN MY HAND

Eddie

I'd never actually written much of anything before. I didn't write about my life until I was 17 years old. That's when I got incarcerated and I wanted people to understand and relate to my experience.

It felt so good. It felt like the paper was listening to me!

I consider myself a writer now. Absolutely. I especially like to write when I'm going through something difficult. It relieves a lot of stress and helps you let go of the anger you feel inside. If a person just writes, he can keep a lot of bad things from happening.

When I write, I feel great, because it's mine. I did it and no one can take it away from me. When people read my work, they tell me things like, "Keep up the good work!" and "Stay strong!" Hearing things like that? It makes me feel like I'm connected to the world.

A Voice to Be Heard

By CM

No matter how many adjectives or verbs
I'm still a voice to be heard
When my vision to you is blurred
I'm still a voice to be heard
While I'm mentally disturbed
I'm still a voice to be heard
When my reason for speaking is absurd
I'm still a voice to be heard
When my pathway is deterred
I'm still a voice to be heard
Even when I can't say a word
I'm still a voice to be heard
So I refuse to let go of this pen!

A Pencil in My Hand

By Immanuel

Put a pencil in my hand
And a sketchpad in front of me
My mind's so focused
It feels like the whole world is under me
My imagination goes wild
And my hand thinks for itself
Listening to what my mind thinks
And stuck on nothing else

When Pencil Meets Paper

By William aka King X

When pencil meets paper

I condemn the facility

Then come back with the remedy

Praying for all enemies

Cuz I'm too profound

Podium speaking I grasp the crowd

Wit' compound word and plenty verbs

Gettin' pension for my proverbs

Cuz when they hit ya it packs a punch like Mossberg

Flyin' round the city I'm a lost bird

In a lost world no longer neat

Just pencil, paper, everything else is obsolete

The pinnacle is here so where should I try and reach

When there's no ripe fruits for me to reap

I'm beyond money, cars, clothes, and sneaks

So I write and out the pencil the graphite leaks

So peep my pedigree when my heart beats them beats

And after pencil meets paper let my mind bleed on beats

My Passion

By Immanuel

The passion I have for writing
Is a feeling of peace and tranquility
The desire to inspire myself ambitiously
A sense of freedom without actually being free
Unlocking my chains with this poetic key
Exceeding beyond this feeling of imprisonment
My mind directs these orchestrated sentences
Creatively creating these lines of inspiration
Carefully planting my seed on this literary plantation
I open the eyes to many who listen
A 19 year-old convict writing from prison
Forever devoted to this paper and pen
My passion…my love…my new best friend

Tick-Tock

By Shakim

How long has it been
Since I've picked up my pen?
How long has it been
Since my words made the world spin?
If they listen, what do you think they'll hear?
Years of pain being drained from my soul, exiting through tears
It's not the job of the misunderstood to make people understand
He's the one misunderstood when he walks the land!
The greats were never pulled out the crowd and put on a throne
They always were unique and stood alone
Often misread and unappreciated
Until they stand tall and their true presence can't be negated
They go from being a shadow to being the light to their people
Even so, they'll never fly with the flock because they were born eagles

Free of Charge

By Makkah Ali

Free of charge

I just ask you pay attention

Because these voices to be heard

Have silently went missing

Somewhere lost behind four walls

In a nightmare called prison

Is there anyone out there

Who cares to spare some time to listen?

I bring a message of hope, encouragement and inspiration

To go after dreams and visions

I write to shed light

My mind is free

It took some time, I was blind, confined

But now I see

Behind the number, behind the crime

I'm still defining me

Not in the past, not in the future

Only in the now, the present, I'm finding me

Voices to be heard, spread the word

Truth from these youth

Food for thought conquers foolish thoughts

A taste for change is what I serve

Photo by Renee Billingslea

TRANSFORMATION

Anthony

Transformation means total and complete change. Leaving the streets was the biggest transformation I could ever have made. When I was in the streets, I was fearless. The only emotion I felt was anger and I was willing to take it out on anybody. I'm ashamed to say it, but I just didn't care about the next person.

From the time I was about eight years old, the streets was my life. My mom was in the streets. I didn't know anything but the streets. For me to want something else? I mean, it just wasn't possible.

It took me going to prison and learning to read for me to want to change. Before that I was illiterate. Everyone in school knew I was illiterate, but they just kept passing me up to the next grade anyway. When I learned to read, that's when I was ready to change. Because once I learned to read, I wanted to comprehend. And once I could comprehend, I just wanted to go further in my education. You know that saying, "Knowledge is Power"? Well, it's true! When I finished my first book, I felt so much power. Like now I knew that couldn't no one get over on me.

When I started reading books about characters like me, that's when it really hit me. I realized, *Man, I'm not the only one going through this!*

I read books about religion and self help books. My favorite book is *As a Man Thinketh*. A lot of times when I read these books, I'm like, *Wow! This is exactly how I feel!*

I remember when I was young, I'd be someplace in public and see a white man, and I wanted to move far away from him because I felt somehow less than him. Once I started reading, I understood why I felt that way. As blacks, we sometimes feel "less than" because of our history. Because of the generations of slavery and discrimination. This feeling gets passed on from one generation to the next. But now I understand and I know I'm not inferior.

I've changed and transformed in so many ways. The one I'm most proud of is that I'm no longer focused on what's going on in the streets. There are people around my way making a lot of money and driving nice cars. There was a time that would have made me feel bad. Like I had to prove myself. But I'm so different now. I don't care. I'm in my own lane, and I'm headed to the very top. I feel at peace.

Chapter 12

I Was You

By Anthony

I was you

I struggled to read

I struggled to write

That's right, I, the person who wrote this poem

Can read and understand these words!

I'm here to let you know

Just cuz you are here in this situation

Doesn't make you or break you

You're young and strong

Mentally, physically, and at heart

And if anyone tells you anything different

Then I'm here to tell you

That only the strong survive

I know this

Because I was you

Then and Now

By LaTrae

Then, I had in my mind that in my near future I would be in a casket
Then, death was a constant thing so things didn't really matter
Then, I used to try to make my momma proud
but my actions only made her sadder
Now, I see life for what it really is
Now, I'm furthering my education
so I can set a good example for my kids
Now, I'm going to live my childhood dreams
of becoming a math teacher
and start calculating dollars
instead of calculating dead
That was then....
This is now

Nothing

By Diquan

I come from nothing
Just like Oprah Winfrey
Since I been locked up
I tried to become something
Instead of nothing

Hold Up, Just Wait!

By David A.

I am running from the fast life

Because I want to see a change

I am running like a speedboat

When I look over my shoulder

I see somebody hating

Telling me I am nothing

They don't want to see me shine

I be maxin' out

But I still know that I'm gonna be something in life

I am running towards the stage

I want the whole world to see me doing my thing

I am running towards that green

That paper

But I want clean money

Not dirty money

I am running towards success

I am running thru the moonlight

Like Neil Armstrong

Looking In The Mirror

By LJ

Coming home to a whirlwind

And I'm trapped in the middle

Drugs, money and violence

Just to name a little

Scared to ask for help

Because I'm afraid of being denied

Thought I would find my own way

But I followed the wrong guide

With each step I took

I didn't realize I was moving backwards

I wish my life was a movie

And I was just the main actor

Instead of manning up and facing my fears

I cut all corners and made it my career

What will I do differently this time?

I ask and I ask

Words aren't nothing but letters put together

Acting upon them is the real task

I figure I should tell on myself

Because I can never tell on anyone else

Maybe the right ears will hear this

And I can find myself some help

Ruined At Birth

By Antonio

Ruined

From the day I was born

From the day I could walk

Running across the street

To the sound of my name being called

Almost got hit by the 96 bus

Ruined

From the day I could talk

Scared to ask questions

Because I didn't want to feel

The belt against my butt

Ruined

From the first day I cried

But no one cared

So I wished I was dead

Ruined

From this day on no longer weak

But strong, mature and ready

To be a changed man and

Not that immature little boy

Born ruined

Trouble Life

By Rakeem

I remember a house full of kids

A heart full of fear

And eyes full of tears

I remember a pocket full of dead presidents

Mom don't have to worry about the rent

My father is incarcerated

So it was the money order I sent

I have a mind full of memories

I remember the hollow tip burning in my flesh

Three inches away from my spine

I could've been paralyzed

The doctor said, *You almost died*

Mom, don't cry

I just smile to cover what's inside

I got my head high into the sky

I was once told, *You are a miracle child*

I just smiled

People loved my style

Yes, back when I was on the streets

I was running wild

Since I been incarcerated I calmed down

I was once lost

But now I'm found

Mango Tree

By Marquis

Imagine how

Being in this damn cage

Used to produce a lot of

Hatred, depression, rage

But 23 and 1 now?*

Naw…

I slow stroke books and savor each page

See, I developed myself to be

Militant minded and scholarly grounded

Maturity, my manhood, Islam….

In jail is where I found it

Forget a rose

I grew a mango tree out of steel and concrete

On solitary confinement, inmates spend 23 hours in their cell and 1 hour out

Courage

By Shawn

Today I found the courage to travel with a sense of direction
Lately I've been traveling in the same circle
Only to find myself stuck in the same position
My courage comes from a voice of the unknown
Speaking words I never heard before
Or are these words from the past that I ignored?
One would never know
But today I found the courage
To change my social crowd
To find new friends—
The same people me and my old friends called different
I've come to realize the only thing that was different
Was our way of thinking from theirs
One was traveling somewhere
While the other was too afraid to travel the unknown
People may criticize me and say I'm different
But I don't care
I found the courage to make a difference

Photo by Robert Lee

THE COLOR OF MY SKIN

Sergio

I remember one really hot day when I was about five years old. All of us little kids were begging the older dudes to turn on the fire hydrant so we could play in the water. They wouldn't do it though. They were trying to sell drugs and argued the customers wouldn't come down the block with the water on. Then this white dude, a firefighter, walked over with a wrench and turned the water on for us. I was really happy. Then I heard the older dudes yelling at him to "take his white a** back to his own neighborhood." That was the day I understood I was black. It was crushing to learn that we were considered different. I thought we were all just human beings.

I had a white friend when I was little. I loved that kid. He and his sister used to invite me to play in their backyard sandbox and they would always let me take a box of Legos home with me. He moved away though. As I grew older, sometimes my friends and I would go down to the mall by the monuments. The black girls would always say hi to us, but when we spoke to the white girls, they pretended we weren't even there. I started to wonder why the white people all lived downtown and we all lived someplace else. My teacher in elementary school, Mr. Gibson taught me that it was very hard to live in America as black people because other people looked down on us. I know some of the dudes started to hate white people. They didn't like seeing white people with everything, when they had nothing. Usually it was the ones who already had grime and hate in their hearts that hated the most.

In prison, race was everything. Eating, going outside, going to school, even when you could use the microwave. It was all determined by your race. Everyone stuck with their own kind. I don't like when people stay with their own kind. Too many people teach their kids that it is supposed to be like this. But I don't believe it. I believe God gave us life to make our own choices.

I am proud of who I am. Being black gives me my confidence and my character. Some people look at me and assume I'm in the streets or that I dropped out of school. When I walk behind a white person they act nervous or they don't hold the door for me when they see that I'm black. It used to make me mad. But now I'm just motivated. It's like a challenge to me. I want people to know that just because my skin color isn't the same as yours doesn't mean I'm better than you, or you're better than me. I want to do something big to better the world. I want to remind people we are all human beings and it will be a better world if people get over this race thing.

Black Male Lost

By Delonte

Black male lost

My seed is paying the cost

Of actions I made

Now he no longer have a daddy

First steps, first words

I missed them all

Never would I be able to recover from that

Stressed, trying not to run my time up

Trying to get back to him

One of the few things I done right in my life

Black male lost

I paid the cost

My life would never be more than a number

Not personality, brains, charm or good looks

Just a number

Nothing more

I'm just another black male lost

100 years ago

By Larry

100 and some years ago
They brought us to this land
100 and some years ago
I couldn't be a man
100 and some years ago
They called us a slave
100 and some years ago
They made us behave
100 and some years ago
They made us figure
100 and some years ago
My name was a n*****
100 and some years ago
They made us wear chains
100 and some years ago
And it's still the same

Lady Growl

By Shahid

Assata ("She Who Struggles")
Shakur ("The Thankful One")

Begin with she who struggles
End with the thankful one
Would never find another
Gave her a taste of dat gun
Just know she still stood
Spoke for dat broken lung
Murder charges dey wrote
Just cuz she smart, she dumb
A G.E.D. grad, spoke with that college tongue
Yeah she my motivation,
Her song is always sung
What she ask for, Vietnam peace
And all my people free
Black Panther roar
Weakened, she spoke so loud
Exile from where, for what
Having a lady growl

Dignity

By Jonas

I want to live my life

In a dignified manner

Elegant and respectable

Discreet but detectable

Morals strong enough to contribute to society

Molding lives for the better

Still down to earth and as real as it gets

Without the poison of hypocrisy, double standards and double lives

I want to lead by example, learn and teach, encourage and influence

I would say that I want to be an upstanding citizen

But that sounds too P.C.

I want to fight against stereotypes

So I'll say

I want to be a dignified black man

Photo by Peter Broyles

MANNIN' UP

Robert

Mannin' up means taking responsibility for yourself and others. It's heavy. It covers everything about the way you live your life.

At the end of the summer when I was 16, there was a warrant out for my arrest. All my friends were talking about where they were going to school in the fall and I remember sitting back and thinking, *I want to go to school! I want to be a good person and be successful!* I knew I couldn't do that if I was on the run. I decided to turn myself in. I needed to deal with what I'd done.

When I was in prison, I would watch these guys blaming everything and everyone except themselves. They would always point the finger, but guess what? You can't blame anybody else for you being in the picture. I ain't never going to blame anyone else. I never did. I was mad at myself because I put myself in that situation. I did it! That's called mannin' up. It's the courage to accept the things you've done and pay the consequences.

I felt remorse for what I did, right away. Yeah, I truly felt bad. I mean, when I really realized what I did and the impact it had? And I'm talkin' deeper than the act itself. I realized it was traumatizing what I did. It could have a long lasting effect on that person. I put myself in that person's shoes and I could feel empathy. I wouldn't want something like that to happen to me. I'm sure it made that person feel antsy and jittery, and who knows? That could have caused them to lash out at someone else. What I did could have just perpetuated even more violence.

I apologized to my victim in the courtroom. I don't know if they forgave me, but I hope so. I believe in forgiving. When you forgive someone, you let go of it and it can't hurt you anymore.

I believe in redemption too. You might do something that is horrible, but that thing doesn't define you. You're human. And as humans, we have the ability to make things right. They might have called me a "jailbird," but I know that isn't who I am. I'm striving to make things right every day. I don't do anything if it might hurt someone. I act responsibly. I am thoughtful. I learn as much as I can learn. And I always look for the good in everything and everyone. I call it being life-bringing. Hell yeah, I believe in redemption. Even though I did something bad, I can say, look at me now!

I Did It

By D'Angelo

I've spent most of my life going through a struggle

I've been at the bottom of the totem pole causing harm and affliction to others

I've been at the lowest part of the food chain

Starving to the point where my body had to eat from my muscles

I've been lied to and deceived, confused and misguided

I've been looked down upon and treated like I was nothing

My smile hurts so bad it feels like I'm not smiling at all

I haven't cried in years and not too often do I complain

I just act nonchalant because if I don't care, I'll feel no pain

I don't really vent because it's no one's business

People don't care anyway, they just pretend to listen

I've been tested and tested left and right

I've fought physically and mentally with all my might

I've laughed in death's face like it was a clown or a joke

I'm as stupid as the porcupine that keeps poking itself

I waited miserably in jail for three and a half years

Working on my character, trying to change gears

All I wanted was a chance to be free, a chance to finally live

I was a caterpillar fresh from a cocoon but right before I could spread my wings

I was told to go back because I chose to partake in yet another criminal scheme

So for the next three to five years I'm going to beat myself up,

And since no one put me down I can't expect no one to help me get up

Redemption

By John

Locked up
Really would never think
That the things I did
I would regret
Know I respect
Myself and others
The bad things
Are temptin' temptin'
But now I'm locked up
I seek redemption

Nocturnal Blue

By LB

This is a color that done so much for me
Good and bad
It made me have a deep hate for red
It gave and took so many of my homies
It gave me a life to live by and to live in
It gave me a block and a street
It made me family and enemies
But the best thing I ever did
Was give it up

Hurting People

By Elijahwon

When you don't have stuff and you need it
You start thinking foolish
And do something to somebody
That didn't do nothing to you
I feel really bad now because of what I did
I feel scared and ashamed
If the law don't get you, God will
So I learned to give back to the people I hurt
And asked God to forgive me
I asked the person that I hurt to forgive me
Think about what you are doing
Stop hurting people and give back

A Lesson Learned

By Hosea

Living my life for the wrong reason
Tryna get it every season
Doing what it takes to stay eating
But hustling for the wrong reasons
Being ignorant to the fact
You can get it without selling crack
Feeling trapped because I am black
Now I can't get this time back
It was a hard lesson learned
That money has a million ways to be earned
If you sit and wait your turn
Life lessons will be learned

Lead by Example

By Gerald

I was told to lead, never to follow

That way you avoid falling in any hollow

'Cause once you fall in that hole

It might not be so easy to get out

The hole probably be so deep

Nobody going to even hear you scream or shout

I'm in a hole right now

But I'm not screaming or shouting

Not showing any sign of displeasure

By frowning or pouting

I'm figuring a way out

'Cause my son is the light

The reason I must have a plan when I get out

So I won't go in the wrong direction

So I will run the correct route

'Cause it's up to me to make him a man

I got to be in his life

Not just give him a little piece or sample

I gotta be the grown man he needs me to be

Not by telling him, but showing him

So I'm going to lead by example!

CHAPTER 15

PM did not want his name used to protect his family's privacy.
**U.S. Immigration and Customs Enforcement*

THE REAL ME

PM*

My family came to the United States when I was 13. My parents had worked hard, and coming to America was their dream. It was hard for me though. I didn't fit in at school and I was really lonely. Then I found the one place where I felt accepted—in the streets. So I started to do bad. I was arrested and ended up in a cell at the DC Jail facing adult charges for burglary. That was really scary. I was 16.

Because of my crime, my entire family had to return to our country. I spent three years behind bars, in federal prison and then at an ICE** facility. When I was released, I was deported.

To this day, my parents have not told the truth about me to anyone. It would cause them horrible shame. They told my little brother I was away at boarding school. I feel sick about what I did. I caused so much pain and trouble. Now my parents have very little money and they struggle to pay the rent. It is my fault. They have always done so much for me.

Coming back to my country and my family though, it felt amazing. I thought, *Finally, I'm out!* I pinched myself so many times! I laid my hand on the concrete. Then I touched my forehead and my heart. I was home.

It has been hard though. The unemployment is very high in my country. My diploma says that I graduated high school in jail. Here, if you have been to prison, they say you are nothing. I pray one day my parents will be able to return to America. Even if I can't go with them. I still have nightmares about the violence I saw and endured in adult prison. The worst part is having nobody I can talk to. Holding it all inside. I know it's not good for me.

Who am I? I am a person who has been through a lot. I am not a bad person. Even though I have almost nothing, when I see a hungry person, I will share my food with them. Sometimes I feel sad like I want to give up. Sometimes we all feel badly though, but we have to fight like a boxer. Not to hurt someone, but put up our hands and fight the situation that we find ourselves in. I will fight until I make it.

It sounds crazy, but it was in the darkness that I discovered myself. It's like I fell in a deep, dark hole. There were hands trying to help me but I just couldn't reach them. When I got out of the hole, I was reborn. The past was gone and I'm new again. Even though it's difficult, I feel blessed to be here with my family and loved ones—having tea every morning with my grandmother and my little brother.

Who am I? I have become a man, but there is still so much that I have to gain in order to become my full self.

My parents tell me I am a good son. I want to hold on to those words forever.

Am I Ugly?

By PM

Eyes closed

Deep inside, I'm pretending to be a free man

It's amazing what I see

So beautiful, wonderful wonderland

My mind is independent, soaring up in the sky

Like a bird with no fear of the world

No matter how hard I try to smell

It's that recycled air that drops me hard back to reality

Like I lost some kind of gravity

I'm still trying not to open my eyes and destroy my hopeful vision

Trying not to believe I'm behind bars like a caged animal in prison

I heard dreams come true if you believe and just keep dreaming

I guess I do have a dream like Martin

But I wonder when it will be startin'

Thousand others' dreams floatin' around in circles

Even hopeless dreams trying to keep up cheer like it's some kind of circus

DA's and judges exiled us from the community

Talking about criminals

Animals that belong in cages

Die in here as we ages

They treat us like we are uglies

Like some kind of hideous creatures

We are still humans for God's sake, leave the judging to our creator

This question repeats in my head and flies in circles

Am I ugly?

But I don't believe it

A Man Incarcerated

By Steven

I am a man incarcerated

Incarcerated in the physical sense

It's necessary to separate those

Who prey on society at large

Or who refuse to obey the laws

A man incarcerated is a guilty man

Who must decide whether he is as lowly as his deed

Or if in fact, he is better than his mistake

A man incarcerated

Is a man who realizes

That his worth is greater

Than the tag of "criminal" that society places upon him

And will find within him the dignity and desire

To become free from mental incarceration

A man incarcerated at this point

Will find a new wealth of thought

That will make him dangerous

To those who have designed the system

That thrives on a pattern of over-incarceration

A man incarcerated

The man who can overcome it is gifted

And will never be imprisoned again mentally or physically

Who am I?

I am a man incarcerated

You Would Know Me If

By Daquan

You see that I'm locked up

And you think I can't make a change in my life

You see that I'm cut-throat and strong

But you don't know me

You would know me if

You knew how hard it was to grow up in my struggle

You would know me if

You knew how I feel when I think people can't help me

You would know me if

You know how much I want my freedom

You see that I talk different and walk different

But you don't know me

You would know me if

You knew that I want something different

You would know me if

You knew how much I have to change in my life

To let my mother see the son she dreamed I would be

Then you would know me

Me/Others

By Robert aka Rah Rah

Me, I'm the one you want to know

Me, I'm the way you want to go

Others are the smoke that loves to be blown

A destructive stimulant that captures your soul

Me, I'm the love that's never dying

An unstoppable force that's forever rising

Others are a dark cloud that possesses no rain

Instead it pours hate and breeds intense pain

Me, I'm the sincerity that resonates with heart and mind

The undeniable truth that crushes lies of any kind

Others are a false reflection of what I really am

A tainted image that longs to be a man

Me, I'm the gift that keeps on giving

The principle of charity that emanates from within

Others are like the desert with its sandy winds

Something that swallows the water and produces nothing

Me, I'm the respiratory system when in the ultimate strife

The device that brings ones from that flat-lined dead state

To the wave of life

My Face

By Derrick

I think my face is only a disguise

To hide the pain that you cannot see

Because if my face was my heart

You'd probably see a different me

Because half of me is bitter

And another half is sweet

But I try to keep

My skeletons buried six feet

I am only 18

But my life is so deep

From the view of my face

My secrets are kept for keeps

Universal Reflection

By Robert aka Rah Rah

My tears fall the same as the rain that drops from the sky
My mind soars the same as the birds that fly
I beam the same as the sun that shines
The heat that cascades down
Is the same warmth projected through my eyes
The rose blooms the same as my capabilities
Like the medicine that heals, yes, I am a remedy
The creator creates the same as I do
Truth builds and destroys the same way lies do
Honor to the trees and also their leaves
The creatures that cultivate the soil
Because I'm thankful to breathe
As one flesh is buried, one's pushed out the womb
As the sun goes down, up comes the moon
The make of my body is majority water
The same as the Earth, which we call Mother Nature
Now is that a coincidence?
Of course it's not
Just a reflection of you

If I Was a Perfect Man

By Demetrius

If I was a perfect man
I would never fall but always stand
For the things I believe and the ones I don't understand
If I was a perfect man
My manners would be different
Like *yes, no,* and *excuse me ma'am*
If I was a perfect man
I would drink out of a glass and not a can
And greet my peers by shaking hands
If I was a perfect man
I would never tell lies to gather fans
Or turn my back against my mans
Or do destructive things to increase or advance
If I was a perfect man
I wouldn't fly just to land
But soar across to prove that I can
Somewhat be a perfect man

Know Thyself

By Terrell

Knowing myself without a doubt
Able to express myself, not havin' to shout
Learning to stay calm and control my anger
Able to become friends with a total stranger
To get here may seem a battle of wits
So here's the secret to doing this
By opening thy mind
And opening thy heart
This, my friend, is the perfect start

Greatest Story Ever Told

By Donald

Lock me up like a dog, and keep me tamed

Worst part about it: kid's got a brain

So now I'm academically correct

Yet dangerously trained

I'm at war with—and in—my own platoon

I can't even see what I've become in my own cocoon

It's going to be okay…They are liars!

If you're talking mistakes, now you're preaching to the choir

Four rights is a circle, so what's four lefts? A square?

I'll just find my own way and meet you there

My opinion doesn't count, and even if it did

I was a disciple for the violence when I was a kid

Now I'm different, only preaching happiness, so…

Are my words only building monuments of nothingness?

I find myself visualizing my life being played over again

Only to realize I'm still in the same spot I've always been

The panic room filled with more cases than it can hold

So what makes me different?

I got the greatest story ever told

The greatest story never told

Is the story you don't tell

Set fire to your flame, don't let 'em keep you in hell

So whether you witness or you listen

Or you read it just to get it

Or if you buy it when it's sold.

This here…is the greatest story ever told

ACKNOWLEDGMENTS

We are grateful for the generous financial support from both individuals and institutions that make our work possible. Free Minds receives and has received funding from the following:

The Advisory Board Company
Capitol Hill Community Foundation
Clark-Winchcole Foundation
The Commonweal Foundation
The Community Foundation for the National
　Capital Region
Crowell & Moring Foundation
Daughters of the American Revolution
DC Commission on the Arts and Humanities
Dealy Foundation
Dworkin Foundation
Eugene and Agnes E. Meyer Foundation
Fullen-Smith Foundation
Global Fund for Children
Harman Family Foundation
Herb Block Foundation
Humanities Council of Washington, DC
International Monetary Fund Civic Program
Irwin Satin Scholarship Fund
Jovid Foundation
Lainoff Family Foundation

Mental Wellness Foundation
Miller & Chevalier Charitable Foundation
Morris & Gwendolyn Cafritz Foundation
National Book Foundation
New York Avenue Foundation
Philip L. Graham Fund
Rockefeller Philanthropy Advisors
Ronald McDonald Foundation House
　Charities® Global
Ronald McDonald Foundation House
　Charities® of Greater Washington D.C.
Rossiter Foundation
Ruddie Memorial Youth Foundation
Share Fund
Snave Foundation
SPARC Foundation, George Washington
　University
SuPau Trust Private Foundation
Takoma Foundation
United Way of the National Capital Area

This book is funded in part from Georgetown University Philosophy and Social Change Grant Program.

Special thanks to photographer Renee Billingslea for donating her time and talent to this project.

Free Minds thanks the DC Department of Corrections, Central Detention Facility, Correctional Treatment Facility, and the wonderful staff and teachers of the DC Public Schools Incarcerated Youth Program who have continued to support our work.

ABOUT US

Free Minds Book Club & Writing Workshop uses books, creative writing, and peer support to awaken DC youth incarcerated as adults to their own potential. Through creative expression, job readiness training, and violence prevention outreach, these young poets achieve their education and career goals, and become powerful voices for change in the community.

Free Minds serves its members through three phases:

- Book Club serves 16- and 17-year-old boys incarcerated at the DC Jail, engaging them in book club discussions, creative writing exercises, and author visits.

- Continuing Support stays connected to members after they turn 18 and are transferred to federal prisons throughout the US by sending them books, birthday cards, letters, a monthly newsletter *Free Minds Connect*, and feedback on their writing. Visit www.freemindsbookclub.org/poetry-blog to read poetry and write comments for the incarcerated poets.

- Reentry Support mentors members upon release by providing paid job readiness and life skills apprenticeships, education and job placements, and a supportive community of fellow Free Minds members.

Community Engagement connects Free Minds members released from prison to diverse audiences from the community through a violence prevention initiative called "On the Same Page." Our members visit schools, universities, juvenile detention facilities, and community groups as "Poet Ambassadors" to share their life experiences and poetry. Participants exchange ideas on the root causes of, and solutions to youth incarceration--a dialogue that promotes healing and nonviolence.

Write Night/Write Lunch brings Free Minds poetry to the community. Volunteers gather to read poetry, meet the Poet Ambassadors, and write feedback for the incarcerated poets.

Since its inception in 2002, Free Minds has reached over 950 youths through their continuum of services. Free Minds is the only organization working with these youths throughout their entire incarceration and when they return home.

For more information or to make a tax-deductible donation, visit our website at
www.freemindsbookclub.org

 FreeMindsDC   freemindsbookclub

Free Minds Book Club & Writing Workshop is a 501(c)3 nonprofit organization.

30136935R00091

Made in the USA
Middletown, DE
14 March 2016